Church World Service

Fifty Years of Help and Hope

Ronald E. Stenning

Foreword by Senator Paul Simon

Published for

Church World Service
A Ministry of the National Council of the Churches of Christ in the U.S.A.
by
Friendship Press • New York

Library of Congress Cataloging-in-Publication Data

Stenning, Ronald E.
Church World Service : fifty years of help and hope / Ronald E. Stenning.
p. cm.
Includes index.
ISBN 0-377-00318-2
1. National Council of the Churches of Christ in the United States of America. Church World Service—History. 2. Church charities—United States—History—20th century. I. Title
BX6.N2S74 1996
361.7'5—dc20 96-43853
CIP

Contents

Acknowledgments

Church World Service expresses its appreciation to Ronald E. Stenning for this fifty-year history of Church World Service and to Senator Paul Simon for writing the Foreword.

The printing and publication of the history has been made possible through the support of The Trull Foundation. The grant is in memory of B. W. Trull of Palacios, Texas, an early and major supporter of CROP.

The book is dedicated by the author to all those staff and volunteers who over the years shared in the ministry of Jesus, who said, "When you do it to the least of these my brethren, you do it unto me," and to those who will carry on the Church World Service ministry of help and hope in the years ahead.

Foreword

During the last fifty years, there has not been a humanitarian crisis in any region of the world where Church World Service has not been present: from the devastation and chaos in Europe after World War II to massive refugee flows in South Asia, from the killing fields of Cambodia to the famines in the Horn of Africa. Church World Service has been there, providing food, medicine, and most of all, hope.

In recent years, the United States Congress has become increasingly unfriendly to foreign aid and our international obligations. Though such programs make up less than 1 percent of the federal budget, they are near the top of the list of proposed budget cuts. In this light, it is refreshing to read the story of people, united by a common spiritual bond, who recognize our responsibility to share our riches with others who happen to be born into less fortunate circumstance. We should do it at home. We should do it in other nations. As you learn of the history and the accomplishments of Church World Service, you realize that we can, and should, make a difference in the lives of people in lands less prosperous than ours.

Ronald Stenning documents the ways in which Church World Service has contributed to alleviating human suffering. Formed in 1946 by religious bodies as a coordinating agency for post-World War II relief efforts, Church World Service mobilized quickly to become, as noted that year by *The New York Times*, "the largest private relief agency." The agency's first appeal in 1946 was for $12 million for relief in Europe and Asia—an astounding amount when you consider that this amount would be the equivalent of $ 94 million today.

Church World Service established its importance not only as a relief provider in other countries, but also in fostering a domestic constituency for these humanitarian efforts. As it drew on the human and financial resources of church members, Church World Service also tapped into the natural resources of our agricultural heartland, creating the Christian Rural Overseas Program (CROP), to coordinate commodity collections and channel Midwest wheat overseas. Church World Service was involved in helping draft the legislation that became Public Law 480. From this beginning, the American farmer's contribution in providing food aid overseas, including the successful PL 480 Food for Peace program, can be traced.

The efforts of Church World Service provide an example of how humanitarian efforts can bridge religious and cultural differences to help people in need. Made up of dozens of Protestant churches in the United States, Church World Service became active in nearly every region of the world. Church World Service reached out to refugees and displaced people in forgotten corners of the world and in places where political considerations may have otherwise hampered governmental relief programs, such as in the Middle East and wartime Vietnam. To cite one example, it formed the Muslim-Christian Brotherhood in the Philippines in the 1960s to coordinate food relief.

This history traces the evolution of the organization from the principle focus on relief to a broader focus on development and on the root causes of hunger and poverty. As the proverb goes, Church World Service sought to help people learn to fish in addition to providing the fish. Ted Kimmel, the first Church World Service worker to die in the line of duty, wrote, "We must not only be content with just handing out food. Our real job is teaching and inspiring." This goal fostered the activities of church groups in recipient countries, such as Japan, where postwar relief activities created church agencies that later helped less developed regions.

Ronald Stenning puts the story of Church World Service in a context of the world events of the last fifty years, giving a keen sense of the breadth and global scale of the organization's activities. We see how the agency adapted to the changing environment, both abroad and here at home, to meet its goals of providing for the less fortunate. The story of Church World Service, however, does not have a final chapter, as it continues to lend a hand to the hungry and destitute in other lands and also in our own. This book provides a solid history of the accomplishments of Church World Service and a peek into where it is headed in the future.

Paul Simon
U.S. Senator
Washington, D.C.

Preface

This is the story of Church World Service, the relief, development, and refugee agency of the National Council of the Churches of Christ in the U.S.A. (NCCC), representing thirty-three Protestant, Orthodox, and Anglican member communions in the United States. It is the story of how, for fifty years men and women, church members across the United States, have taken seriously the words in the twenty-fifth chapter of Matthew's Gospel, "When you did it to the least of these my brethren, you did it unto me."

The desolation that existed in Europe and much of Asia during the years immediately following World War II is almost impossible to imagine five decades later. Scores of cities and towns had been reduced to rubble. Thousands of families were living in tents, shacks, and in the remains of bombed-out buildings. Hunger was pervasive; in Europe a searing drought in the summer of 1946 had decimated the anticipated wheat harvest.

Church people in the United States, although many had lost sons, daughters, and relatives in the war, looked for ways to share their bountiful harvests with the hungry and the destitute of Europe and Asia. Volunteer agencies stood ready to help in ways that governments could not. Church World Service was founded in response to those crying human needs.

Over the years those needs have changed and so has the nature of the CWS response to them. It has gone from immediate postwar relief to long-term social and economic development programs.

• From providing food, clothing, and medicines in the days immediately following a disaster, to participating in the creation of Interfaith Disaster Response organizations that help people put their lives back together.

• From merely sharing information about the existence of world hunger, to in-depth education programs about the root causes of hunger and poverty and to advocating public policies to relieve these problems.

• From resettling refugees from post-war Europe, to finding new homes and new lives for refugees from Southeast Asia, Haiti, and Cuba.

In the past fifty years Church World Service has grown from its largely rural roots to become a truly global organization, active in more than seventy countries around the world. Nevertheless, in spite of all the changes that have occurred, the goals of CWS have remained the same: to help the victims of natural disasters, refugees from wars and civil conflicts, the hungry, and those for whom survival is a daily challenge; to help people help themselves; to provide the necessities of life, to free people from malnutrition and disease, and enable them to participate in the decisions that affect their own lives.

All that Church World Service has done over the past fifty years has been based on the conviction that the lives of all in the human family are of equal value, and in the hope that through its efforts CWS can help make possible a more humane global society.

The story of Church World Service, in essence, covers the latter half of the twentieth century, fifty years that experienced unprecedented change in most aspects of world affairs. Once powerful nations declined in importance, dozens of new nations declared their independence, a cold war divided the world into East and West while a hot war tore at the fabric of the United States. The story of CWS is a look at five decades of reaching out to help relieve the suffering and human needs of those caught up in the massive changes that were taking place in the world.

This history recounts the story of Church World Service in the context of those world events, for it is only in understanding where and why such compassionate response to human need is necessary that the story of CWS makes sense.

Ultimately, it is a story of relationships. Working through colleague agencies and overseas churches, CWS has consistently encouraged self-determination and self-reliance. As part of a global network of similar national church service agencies, CWS has worked in partnerships and consortia in such places as Cambodia and the Horn of Africa. Underlying all its efforts has been the practice of turning over its activities and programs to local people and local church-related organizations when possible.

Through the years Church World Service has been undergirded by the dedication and commitment of thousands of volunteers in the United States. In 1946, people loaded boxcars with food and other essentials for shipment overseas; families opened their homes and their communities to refugees from war-torn Europe and Asia. Today the volunteers who organize and participate in CROP events still make it possible for CWS to respond to human need overseas and to the needs of the hungry and homeless in this country. It is the volunteer Disaster Response Consultants who go into communities devastated by natural disasters to help CWS and its supporting congregations respond in appropriate ways. Still, church people help refugees find new lives in a new land.

This history is written for the general reader, for those who have been part of Church World Service and CROP over the years, and for those who want to know more about what the U.S. churches have done in response to human need in the last half century. It is not, for the most part, based on primary sources. Typically such primary sources were not available. Much of what is included here comes from dozens of letters and documents sent to me by staff, both former and present, and from committee members who helped shape and govern CWS through the years. It draws on historical accounts written in past years and graphic accounts from men and women still serving overseas. It is a work of storytelling and of interpretation. However, it is a faithful reflection of the seminal events, decisions, and actions that have made Church World Service what it is today.

The story of Church World Service is the story of people: of thousands of unknown and unheralded volunteers, of individuals who organize CROP events in communities all across America, of staff people who over the years have gone into lonely and dangerous places to bring the love of Christ into situations of human need, and of colleagues around the world who have put their own lives on the line and have helped make it all possible.

Space does not permit the naming of everyone whose individual stories make up the history of Church World Service. However, those mentioned represent all those men and women who have been faithful servants of the one who said "I have come to preach good news to the poor" and who have made Church World Service a reflection of that love.

What follows is their story. The story of Church World Service: Fifty Years of Help and Hope.

Dayton, Ohio
September 30, 1996

And the king will answer them, "Truly I tell you, just as you did it to one of the least of these who are members of my family, you did it to me."

Matthew 25:40 NRSV

We must build a new world, a far better world—one in which the eternal dignity of [all humanity] is respected.

President Harry S. Truman

Part One

1946–1956

The year was 1946. The bloodiest and most destructive war in human history was over. Millions had been killed. Much of Europe and large parts of Asia were in ruins. Hundreds of thousands of people were hungry and homeless, some in camps, others carrying all their worldly possessions wandering from one place to another looking for food and shelter. There had been refugees in the past but nothing to compare with the numbers of displaced persons and refugees during and following the years of World War II.

In the United States, the transition from war to peace was an experience for American society almost as convulsive as the transition from peace to war four years earlier. Thousands of service people were being discharged from the armed forces and returning to civilian life. After years of war, the demands on the economy were for sufficient housing, appliances, automobiles, and countless other commodities to meet the needs not only of returning veterans but also those who had experienced shortages of all kinds on the home front. High prices and the scarcity of meat, nylon stockings, new cars, and decent housing plagued almost everyone.

It was also a year of social turmoil. Never had the country experienced such labor and business confrontations. Loosed from wartime wage and price restrictions, the country faced the possibility of runaway inflation and crippling strikes in major industries. In May 1946, the nation's railroads and the soft coal industry threatened to strike over wages and working conditions. The strikes were averted only at the last moment through direct intervention by the President.

Politically, the midterm elections of that year ended sixteen years of unbroken Democratic control of Congress, while on the international scene, 1946 began with the United Nations opening its first Assembly in London. Both the country and the world obviously faced mountainous new obstacles in the years immediately ahead. It was in that kind of world that Church World Service came into existence.

I

Long before 1946, churches in Europe and the United States had been deeply involved in service to people in need. Church groups had provided food and other essentials to thousands who suffered and perished from hunger in the great China famines of the nineteenth century. They had formed relief groups in 1918 to help rebuild churches damaged or destroyed in World War I. In 1922, American and Swiss church members had met in Copenhagen to establish the European Central Bureau for Interchurch Relief. In 1939, the Federal Council of Churches (FCC) and the Foreign Missions Conference created a Committee on Foreign Relief Appeals in the Churches, while in 1944, they formed The Church Committee for Relief in Asia. Later another organization, the Church Committee for Overseas Relief and Reconstruction (CCORR) served as an umbrella agency and included the YMCA, YWCA, the American Bible Society, the World Student Christian Federation, and the American Friends Service Committee.

By the mid-1940s, the proliferation of relief agencies and other groups caused the situation to become increasingly complicated. On May 4, 1946, the Federal Council of Churches, the Foreign Missions Conference, and the American Committee of the World Council of Churches jointly established Church World Service to be the relief and service arm of the churches. Member denominations were invited to appoint representatives to its governing board and seventeen did so. In addition, twelve other organizations entered into an affiliate relationship.[1] Thus the first inclusive, ecumenical, and coordinating instrument for overseas relief and reconstruction in the history of the Protestant churches in the United States came into being. The name "Church World Service" was in many ways an inspired choice as it brought together the three words that described the program on which it was about to embark: the Church in Service in the World. A. L. Warnshuis, Secretary of the International Missionary Council of the FCC, was named its first director.

The plan was for Church World Service to be the coordinating agency in which issues could be discussed, and decisions agreed to and carried out. CWS was also to be a means of making joint appeals for funds to carry on the service work of the churches. A *New York Times* article in late 1946 announced a CWS appeal with a goal of $12 million to be "used for relief and reconstruction in both Europe and Asia." The Times article described Church World Service as "the largest private agency distributing foreign relief."

When CWS was established, it had assumed responsibility for eight material aid centers in the United States belonging to CCORR and a ninth center that had been opened by the Southern Baptists. From those centers, in the first few months of its existence, CWS shipped forty-eight carloads of food and four million pounds of clothing to people overseas. In 1946, CWS provided 80 percent of all relief goods shipped from U.S. voluntary agencies to Europe and Asia.

Also in those first few months, Church World Service was deeply involved in refugee work. With the War Relief Service of the National Catholic Welfare Congress, CWS appealed to the Intergovernmental Commission for Refugees (the group responsible for displaced persons camps in Europe) for a far more expansive resettlement policy, and one that would use voluntary agencies for resettlement of refugees. Before the end of 1946, CWS had resettled 1,488 refugees in thirty-two cities and 124 communities in the United States. It also had thirty-six staff people overseas, active in immigration and refugee-related programs, working with displaced persons, returning prisoners of war, and feeding thousands of hungry children.

Food shortages were so acute in 1946 that Great Britain had to reinstate wartime bread rationing because of a lack of wheat. Meanwhile, that same year, farmers in the United States harvested a record 1,123,000,000 bushels.[2] Faced with those stark realities, people in many parts of rural America began to think of ways to share their harvest with the starving people of Europe. Church World Service called a meeting of representatives of Councils of Churches in the wheat belt who voted unanimously that "the Protestant churches of the wheat belt should engage in a 'Wheat Relief Project' at the time of the 1947 wheat harvest." Wheat for Relief committees were set up in Oklahoma, Kansas, Colorado, Nebraska, and both Dakotas. They shipped the first boxcar of wheat from Oklahoma in July. Hearing of that effort, the columnist Drew Pearson wrote to Charles Luckman of the Citizens Food Committee in the White House, suggesting the idea of a Friendship Train to cross the United States, picking up carloads of donated food stuffs as it moved eastward, "inspiring housewives and farmers of the nation to spare a bag of flour or a bushel of wheat and bring it down to the Friendship Train as their contribution toward friendship with the people of Europe." That Friendship Train created much interest among those who were looking for ways to move some of their harvested wheat to ports for overseas shipment and who wanted to, in Pearson's words, "convince the people of Europe that this food comes not from the United States Government but from every dinner table in America—a sacrifice from the American people to their less-fortunate fellows."

Encouraged by the success of the Wheat for Relief appeal, Church World Service authorized a general appeal for farm commodities under the name Christian Rural Overseas Program (CROP). M. R. Zigler, executive director of the Brethren Service Committee, suggested that any rural appeal should have a Midwest base if there was any hope of its being successful. When the decision was made to create CROP, John Metzler Sr., then director of the Brethren Service Center in New Windsor, Maryland, was appointed national director. With a grant from the Brethren Service Committee, and a corresponding grant from the Evangelical and Reformed World Service Commission, he opened the first national CROP office in the Brethren Bethany Seminary in Chicago, using one of the boys' dormitory rooms as the first CROP office. Ruth Milner became national field director, and soon state CROP offices were set up in Kansas, Illinois, Iowa, and Oklahoma to coordinate the commodity collection. Ken McDowell, then a student at Bethany Seminary, became the first business manager of CROP. He later became a Church of the Brethren official and long-time member of the CWS Unit Committee. He recalls that in those days, "CWS was the jewel of ecumenical cooperation . . . Denominational members of the CWS Committee were committed to the idea that the needs of the world were so great that only through combining our resources could we make a significant contribution." Bill Cline was the Public Relations Director and was instrumental in publicizing the new organization throughout the Midwest and Western states.

The Drew Pearson Friendship Train became the prototype for CROP-sponsored Friendship Trains operating through the Southwest and the northern wheat states. The largest effort, the Abraham Lincoln Friendship Train, which started across country on Lincoln's birthday, February 12, in 1948, was not one train but several. Nebraska had contributed 110 carloads of grain. South Dakota and Iowa each provided some thirty cars, with additional cars coming from Kansas, Colorado, Wyoming, North Dakota, and Minnesota. The Illinois train equaled that of Nebraska, with 110 carloads. From Michigan came nineteen carloads of split beans and one of wheat, while Ohio shipped more than forty carloads of grain. As in many other places, the Ohio contribution was sent off following a dedication service at the state fair grounds attended by the governor of the state.

By the end of 1948, in at least twenty-three states, CROP was assembling Christmas Trains. Between 2,000 and 2,500 freight cars loaded with gifts of grain, beans, rice, meat, cotton, and other products of U.S. farms were shipped to ten different ports in the United States where dedication services were held at the same hour on Christmas Day. Besides the trains, there were also "CROP Friendship Food Ships" that were loaded out of Chicago, Toledo, Philadelphia, Baltimore, and Houston before sailing for overseas.

During 1948, CWS was joined in sponsoring CROP by Lutheran World Relief (LWR) and the Catholic Rural Life Conference, making it a truly ecumenical effort. The success of CROP in those early years was due largely to the dedication of local volunteers who not only contributed commodities but also their time and effort to prepare shipments. Volunteers sent out special mailings alerting the public to the need for help in alleviating the hunger and suffering in Europe and Asia. In that way additional funds were raised.

II

With the devastation of war still evident in much of Europe, Secretary of State George Catlett Marshall, with the support of President Harry Truman, announced at a Harvard commencement an ambitious plan to help the nations of Europe recover and rebuild. While this Marshall Plan made billions of dollars available for rehabilitation and reconstruction in Europe, conditions in other parts of the world continued to create major human problems, including massive numbers of refugees, especially on the Indian subcontinent, in Asia, and in the Middle East.

After granting India independence, the British had withdrawn from the subcontinent in 1947, and the country was partitioned into Hindu India and Islamic Pakistan. That partition was accomplished at the cost of a million lives. In all, about 10 million people crossed the India-Pakistan border in both directions, and approximately one out of ten died because of violence, sickness, or hunger. Church World Service was there in the midst of that horror and helped to bring aid to the suffering of both nations.

Church World Service received national recognition when a subcommittee of the U. S. House of Representatives, after an intensive study of private assistance, cited CWS for its response to the need for emergency relief supplies of medicines and special foods in India and Pakistan. The congressional report said that, within forty-eight hours CWS "had sent more than $70,000 worth of penicillin, antitetanus serum, and other medical supplies to India by airfreight and placed an additional order for $100,000 worth of food and medical supplies to be sent immediately."[3]

In Asia, there had begun a flood of one million refugees from China into Hong Kong, while more than two million North Koreans had fled into South Korea. In Hong Kong, Church World Service responded with massive shipments of food, clothing, and medicines. Thus began a long involvement for CWS in Hong Kong that resulted in an editorial in *The Christian Century* that said, "Church World Service is doing work which would justify everything the American churches put into it, even if it did nothing else in the whole world."[4]

The Middle East has long been a center for the world's major religions. Judaism, Christianity, and Islam all had their beginnings and early history there. Churches established in Apostolic times have existed for almost two centuries. Nevertheless, the Middle East has also been the scene of conflicting interests growing out of different historical origins, traditions, and languages.

In 1948, a cable to Charles P. Taft, President of the Federal Council of Churches, described the "appalling facts of the Palestine refugee problem" and appealed for help. The first response came from Church World Service announcing a shipment of clothing and the issuing of an appeal on behalf of the refugees.[5] Working with the International Christian Committee for the Relief of Arab Refugees, Church World Service provided food, milk powder, medicine, and vitamins to refugees in Lebanon, Syria, Jordan, and Jewish Palestine.[6] It also helped provide meals through seven soup kitchens and four milk centers that had been set up in Jerusalem.

As early as 1946, CWS was already involved in helping shape public opinion and public policies. A. L. Warnshuis had challenged that "the churches must help stir up that public opinion that will compel governments to give more adequate attention to human needs." Roland Elliot of the CWS refugee program, in cooperation with the Displaced Persons Committee of the American Council of Voluntary Agencies (ACVA), suggested principles for the resettlement of refugees by voluntary agencies, and with other agencies stressed the importance of speed in resettling refugees from war-torn Europe. Earlier, President Truman had issued a Presidential Directive to admit 40,000 war refugees into the United States, with U.S. citizens signing "corporate affidavits" for each refugee guaranteeing that he or she would not become a public charge. CWS submitted several thousand of those documents, and in 1946 and 1947 resettled almost 2,500 refugees under the provisions of that program.

The Displaced Persons Act of 1948 opened up new opportunities, and by 1949 the resettling of displaced persons had become an extremely important activity of CWS. In that year, 7,563 refugees were brought to the United States by CWS and resettled by church people in communities across the country.

During its first full year of activity, Church World Service sent to Europe $8,828,190 of assistance, including contributed commodities valued at $5,468,325. The amount sent to Asia was $4,898,534, of which $2,342,362 was cash and the rest supplies.[7] A large portion of the commodities sent overseas was collected by CROP volunteers and donated by church members.

******

People like Glenn Hulsebus of Iowa, Gerald Young of Ohio, and Kenneth Locke of Nebraska all still remember what it was like in those early years. Glenn Hulsebus writes of meeting with Drew Pearson when Pearson brought a train through Iowa "collecting grain from the Midwest to be shipped to the countries of Europe." Gerald Young was the person hired to promote the idea of the Friendship Trains. His records show that it cost "7 cents on the dollar to promote, gather the grains and to get them to a port of embarkation." Among his mementos is a letter from the Department of State announcing plans for "six ten-minute programs" to be broadcast on the Voice of America telling the story of CROP and the distribution of food. He also has an endorsement of CROP by Trygve Lie, first Secretary-General of the United Nations, who praised the organization in "lessening the acute need in other lands." Meanwhile, Kenneth Locke was an organizer in several Nebraska counties and remembers how "the ecumenical spirit was so strong that no one cared what denomination I belonged to."[8]

III

Although meeting human need in other parts of the world and resettling refugees in the United States continued to be the main focus of CWS, its concerns also included the rebuilding of churches and church life in countries devastated by war. In 1947 it arranged for twenty-seven European theological students to be brought to the United States to study at thirteen seminaries. It also made possible the printing and shipping of Christian books and papers in several languages to countries in both Europe and Asia.

By 1949 CWS was active in twenty-three countries and CROP in twenty-five states in the United States. It was also the year the One Great Hour of Sharing (OGHS) began, an ecumenical effort that became a major promotional activity of CWS. Recognizing that strong financial support from the denominations and church members was vital to enable Church World Service to adequately respond to what was happening in the world, in a national radio address, The Rt. Rev. Henry Knox Sherrill, Presiding Bishop of the Episcopal Church and the first President of the National Council of Churches, called for such an ecumenical undertaking. Church World Service supplied 75,000 posters and three million offering envelopes to the churches that first year.

In addition to the massive worldwide refugee crisis to which CWS was attempting to respond, a severe famine began in India. Church World Service shipped CROP foods there in large amounts to be used in feeding programs for women and children. Meanwhile, CWS was still involved in activities made necessary by the war in the Pacific. Five years after the war, rehabilitation and reconstruction was going slowly in Okinawa and the Philippines. Large areas of those countries were still in shambles. Denominational missionaries were extremely helpful in areas where CWS sent relief supplies, and where no missionaries were available a CWS representative had to accompany the aid. CWS sent food, medicines, and educational supplies to Okinawa with a CWS representative to oversee the program, as there were so few Christian missionaries in Okinawa at the time. The Philippines received similar relief supplies, and CWS-related medical units were sent to the islands of Luzon, Mindanao, and Panay.

Rehabilitation efforts were going ahead in Japan. In 1949, more than three million pounds of Church World Service supplies went to 2,000 institutions in that country: orphanages, baby clinics, schools, hospitals, and old people's homes. More than 170,000 children and adults received assistance regularly.[9] In comparison, the picture in Korea was not as encouraging. People were still fleeing from the North. Adequate shelter was scarce, and there was a great lack of warm clothing and nourishing food. It was estimated that out of a population of twenty million in South Korea, more than seven million were refugees. In response to the needs there, CWS sent seven hundred tons of food and clothes valued at $632,945, as well as $90,389 in funds.

A change in leadership had occurred in Church World Service. Dr. A. L. Warnshuis had retired and was succeeded on a temporary basis by Canon Almon R. Pepper, Director of the Department of Christian Social Relations of the Episcopal Church, and Herbert C. Lytle Jr., a Methodist minister. Canon Pepper was in charge of policy and Dr. Lytle of administration until a full-time director was named.

IV

The end of the forties and the beginning of the fifties were years of significance on the world scene and for the American churches.

In Asia, a communist republic had been set up in North Korea. The Nationalists had been driven from the mainland and a new government established in China. In Vietnam, opposition to the government was on the rise. Then in the middle of 1950 the Korean war began. As the fighting swept southward, CWS lost a quantity of supplies in Seoul and Inchon. Remaining supplies, in Pusan, were used to help thousands of refugees in the country. Because of a shortage of funds to meet all the demands placed upon it, and to have sufficient funds to send to Korea, a difficult decision was made to end relief work in the Philippines, Malaysia, and Thailand.[10]

Organizational changes affecting Church World Service were also taking place. In 1950, the denominations merged several organizations and agencies to form the National Council of the Churches of Christ in the U.S.A. (NCCCUSA). Primary among the merged organizations were the Federal Council of Churches, the Home Missions Council, and the International Council of Religious Education. In the process, CWS became a department of the newly-formed National Council.

It was a time of crisis in many ways for CWS. Postwar emergency funds from the denominations had begun to run out. Funds available were often designated for specific purposes, leaving insufficient funds for administration. The reorganization itself was taking a great deal of staff time that could have been used to carry out programs. Finally, though substantial numbers of refugees were eligible for resettlement in the United States, funds were not available.

Also, apparently some denominations were having second thoughts about Church World Service, wondering if it should not begin to phase itself out of existence. One denominational leader said CWS was "about to fold up." Some mission boards objected to CWS, believing it was duplicating or in time would duplicate their work.[11] However, when the threat to its continued existence became known, CWS received support from lay people and clergy across the country. One national publication wrote, "Millions of church members have found in CWS a new faith in the future of cooperative Christianity . . . now that CWS has been transferred to the NCCC it must be kept alive and given new strength for the great tasks before it."[12]

Church World Service was continued but on a much lesser scale. It was agreed that it was to have a small permanent structure and initiate programs only on a scale that denominations and mission boards would support. Fred W. Ramsey, a retired Ohio lay member with broad experience with voluntary organizations, was brought in as director of CWS to oversee its reorganization and the paring down of its activities and personnel. Meanwhile, CWS carried on its work as best it could, including its theological scholarship program, now bringing students to the United States from Asia and Europe.

Church World Service, along with other agencies, had waged a long battle to obtain Congressional approval for the resettlement of a responsible share of refugees in the United States. When immigration bars began to fall, CWS could respond to the appeals of the Department of Inter-Church Aid and Service to Refugees of the World Council of Churches that it receive and resettle more refugees. Even in the time of retrenchment and reduction of staff, refugee-related activities continued to absorb enormous staff time and energies. With the help of the denominations, 19,300 refugees were resettled in 1950, and 23,142 in 1951. By the end of 1951, 250,000 displaced persons had come to the United States. Some had come under CWS sponsorship, and some under the sponsorship of other church and secular groups.

Changes were also taking place in other parts of Church World Service. In 1952, Lutheran World Relief and the Catholic Rural Life Conference withdrew from sponsorship of CROP. Church World Service again became the sole sponsor, and the national CROP office was moved from Chicago to Elkhart, Indiana. However, contributors of funds and commodities to CROP were allowed to continue to designate their gifts to those other organizations, a practice that continues today. From 1947 to 1952, donations through CROP totaled approximately 5,500 railway boxcars of farm products, with hundreds of thousands of dollars worth of commodities and other gifts being credited to Catholic Relief Services, Lutheran World Relief, the Mennonite Central Committee, and Heifer Project International.

Although the initial emphasis in CROP was on the contribution of commodities, some cash was also received. With the knowledge and approval of donors, some donated commodities were sold and the funds used to purchase needed commodities in other locations to speed shipping. In that way CROP bought carloads of particularly needed food commodities, such as rice, wheat, processed soybeans, and edible oils.

Church World Service and CROP leaders quickly recognized that relief activities were not enough. They understood the desire of people to become self-sufficient and began using some donated funds to purchase and send tools, seeds, building materials, and windmills overseas. In so doing, they had begun to shift the emphasis away from pure relief to programs of social and economic development.

In the early fifties there were also changes in the leadership of

CWS and CROP. With the reorganization completed, Fred Ramsey again retired, and Wynn C. Fairfield, an executive of the Congregational Christian Church, became executive director of CWS. John Metzler Sr. accepted a position on the staff of the World Council of Churches (WCC) in Geneva, and Albert W. Farmer, a former Iowa regional director, became National Director of CROP.

V

By the beginning of 1952, there were five million North Korean refugees in South Korea, one million Arab refugees in and around Palestine, one million Chinese refugees in Hong Kong, and unnumbered refugees in India and Pakistan.[12] The numbers continued to increase, but that was also the year that the Displaced Persons Act of 1948, under which CWS had resettled more than 51,000 persons, expired. Also in that year, the International Refugee Organization (IRO) of the United Nations was disbanded. To further complicate matters, the passage—over the veto of President Truman—of the restrictive McCarran-Walter Immigration and Nationality Act in June 1952 resulted in a comprehensive reorganization of the immigration and naturalization laws of the United States.

The World Council of Churches cut its refugee staff at the beginning of 1952, but was forced to increase it again in May. Church World Service ended its resettlement program in June of that year, but it too was compelled to start an immigration service within a month. The human situation and the still pressing need of refugees could not be ignored.

By 1953, it appeared that emergency legislation was the only way to provide relief to thousands of people awaiting resettlement. To that end, the Refugee Relief Act (RRA) was passed, and the first RRA arrival sponsored by CWS came to the United States on September 22, 1954.

While staff devoted much time and effort to refugee concerns, the demands upon CWS to provide relief in disaster situations continued. Floods in Holland, England, and Japan had left many homeless. An earthquake that devastated parts of Greece, floods and drought in various places in India, and disastrous fires in Korea and Hong Kong were some events to which CWS responded and that strained its financial resources again.

However, by the early fifties, it seemed that denominational support for CWS was on the rise. CWS grew in strength because church people all over America made it their way for meeting crises that occurred in the world community regularly. Church members had come to put their trust and their confidence in Church World Service. Stockpiles of disaster relief supplies were being located in strategic places in the United States. When a disaster struck, shipments could be underway immediately, often more quickly than the government in the affected area could provide them.

Nineteen fifty-four was a watershed year in that the U.S. government made surplus commodities available to church and other voluntary agencies for distribution. Earlier, when surplus grains began to pile up in storage, Clyde Rogers, director of the Town and Country Department of the Ohio Council of Churches, and a member of the Ohio CROP Committee, went to Washington and met with representatives of the Department of Agriculture to discuss releasing grain to voluntary organizations for shipment overseas. He was told that if the agencies could distribute it, the government would release some for them. When national CROP agreed it could be done, the first shipment of government surplus grain to be distributed by a voluntary agency was on the way.

Bolstered by the success of that first shipment, staff of the Ohio CROP office under Regional Director Margaret Brugler, along with the assistance of people from the Ohio CROP Board, Clyde Rogers, and the Department of Rural Sociology and Agriculture Economics of Ohio State University, wrote the first draft of what was to become Public Law 480 (PL 480), the Food for Peace Bill. That draft was presented to Senator Hubert H. Humphrey, who then introduced it, and it became the law of the land.

From the beginning there were those in the churches who were uncomfortable with accepting commodities under PL 480, concerned that the use of government commodities might give the government some control over the agency. That concern was to surface throughout the next ten years, until a major CWS consultation was held to study the issues involved in church participation in the distribution of public commodities. At the time of the passage of PL 480, though, the CWS executive director, Wynn Fairfield said that with proper support from the denominations, CWS could ship and distribute additional surplus commodities valued at $60 million a year. He held that CWS had had wide experience since its founding in 1946, and helped by missionaries and people from local churches overseas, it could handle that increase without any of the problems of government control some were predicting.

Using PL 480 and CROP commodities, between 1954 and 1964 CWS shipped 2.5 billion pounds of commodities valued at $250 million to some fifty countries. The Material Aid Department of CWS, under the direction of Melvin Myers, had developed an overseas shipping capability equal in skill and capacity to that of a large export firm. By the early 1950s it was arranging ocean freight and inland transportation, securing export licenses, negotiating insurance policies, and making arrangements with foreign governments for CWS and for the denominations that used CWS for shipping to their own missionaries, schools, and hospitals throughout the world.

Nineteen fifty-four was also a significant year for Church World Service in other ways: it became involved in Vietnam for the first time. CWS joined the Mennonite Central Committee in sending food and other relief supplies to meet the acute need among refugees from the north. That program was ended when its immediate relief objective was realized, but also because NCCC member communions had no ongoing relationships within Vietnam. Few probably realized how active CWS would become in Vietnam in the years ahead.

Meanwhile, CWS had entered into a church-related relief effort in Taiwan. In 1955, "Taiwan CWS" was organized and became the center for the distribution of CWS and Lutheran World Relief clothing. Most of it went to people in serious need, including war widows and children. That year, 448,000 pounds of clothing were shipped to Taiwan. Then, with the availability of PL 480 food commodities there was an enormous expansion of the program. In a conference between Protestants, Roman Catholics, and officials of the U.S. government about how those commodities were to be used, it was agreed that the feeding program would be limited to one million needy persons. Eventually the size of the program and the availability of large amounts of food and other commodities caused it to spin out of control. It became clear to CWS officials that Christian missions on the island opposed the feeding programs because of the problems involved, and after much soul-searching, the executive committee of CWS announced that the agency would "gradually withdraw its mass feeding program in Taiwan."[13] Although it took several years, that withdrawal was finally accomplished.

Boyd Lowry, Asia area director and later executive director of Coordination in Development (CODEL), said that in the decade between 1955 and 1965 CWS learned many of its most valuable lessons. Certainly there were lessons in the Taiwan experience for CWS. At least two of them were that CWS should maintain continuity of leadership in programs like Taiwan, and that CWS must protect its integrity and identity in its relationships with governments, both United States and foreign. For Church World Service, Taiwan was a good teacher.

In April 1955, a major earthquake occurred in the southern Philippines causing massive destruction and considerable loss of life. Assistance was sent by CWS to the National Council of Churches in the Philippines, the partner agency of CWS. Church members in the Philippines were involved in distributing relief supplies to Muslim and Christian people in the devastated areas.

VI

The story of Tanya Chwastov has been told elsewhere, but it deserves a place in this history because it illustrates a fundamental truth about Church World Service: the welfare of an individual child can be just as important as any program involving hundreds if not thousands of people.

Tanya had been born in the United States. Her father was a refugee from Russia and her mother, his common-law wife, a refugee from Yugoslavia. Church World Service had helped resettle both parents. When the parents separated the father wanted to return to Russia and take the child with him. The mother objected, as did Church World Service.

In 1956, it was believed that Russian agents were putting pressure on refugees to return to Russia, Tanya's father among them. Alerted that Chwastov was under pressure from those agents, a CWS representative visited him to tell him that he would be protected and not to be afraid. Although he gave the CWS representative the impression he wanted to stay in the United States, he soon disappeared leaving all his belongings behind. He was hidden for several days by Russian officials and was then seen boarding the Queen Mary in the company of Russian agents, carrying the young Tanya.

Immigration officials searched the ship before it sailed but found no sign of the girl or her father. Newspapers called it a kidnaping, and soon a Senate committee investigated and accused Soviet officials of participating in the abduction of the child.

R. Norris Wilson, who had become executive director of CWS, flew to London and, with the help of British friends, brought an action in the British courts to decide if the child should be returned to her mother. The father then attempted to flee England with the child on a Russian ship but was taken ashore and made to appear in court. The decision of the court favored the mother, who brought the child back to the United States. The story of

Tanya was followed in the newspapers of two continents for several months. CWS had made the point that there were people and organizations in the United States who were ready to stand up and protect the very young and seemingly helpless of the world.

******

It was in those early years that a young volunteer, John Backer, first became a part of the Church World Service Immigration and Refugee Program. He recalls how, in 1950, he would go to the piers in New York where an army transport ship chartered by the United States would arrive from Germany. Those transports were loaded with displaced persons from Europe, including usually 200 to 300 sponsored by CWS. He helped those persons through customs, helped with baggage transfers, and took them by bus to Pennsylvania Station where they were placed on trains to their final destination. John Backer recently retired after thirty-eight years on the staff of the refugee program he joined almost five decades ago.

Elvin Frantz, another long-time staff member of CWS/CROP recalls how, as a young college graduate in 1946, he was asked to help get wheat contributed for a new organization, the Christian Rural Overseas Program, which became known as CROP. Borrowing a truck, he drove from farm to farm collecting wheat. After he had collected enough for a carload in Colorado, a large banner was made proclaiming where the wheat was destined. A railside service was held dedicating the wheat for hungry people overseas. Elvin, also now retired, spent the rest of his working life on the staff of that "new organization."

Meanwhile, on the other side of the world, a young agricultural missionary was working in Central India. Bill Whitcomb had never heard of Church World Service or CROP. Nevertheless, he did know that the people in the villages where he worked were in dire need of food.

He remembers the day that a railway wagonload of wheat arrived that had been sent from CWS for use in a hospital and for distribution to the hungry people in the area. He also recalls that the wheat arrived full of weevils, in fact so full that the bags were actually moving. However, the wheat was still eatable by the country standards of the time. He tells of taking the hospital jeep loaded with four bags of wheat to a village where most people were in considerable distress because of severe drought and crop failure and distributing the wheat to them.

That was Bill Whitcomb's first awareness of CWS and CROP. But after some twenty years in India, he returned to the United States to become a regional CROP director in Wisconsin for many more years.

The stories of people like John Backer, Elvin Frantz, and Bill Whitcomb are at the heart of the story of Church World Service.

Dedication of CROP Friendship Food Shipment from several Midwest states. Chicago, Illinois. United Nations Day, 1950

W. Cline/CWS

CWS/CROP Archives

"CROP Friendship Food Ship" sailing for Europe with food from U.S. farmers. 1949

Gene's Candid Studio/River Falls, Wisc.

Representatives of Church World Service, Lutheran World Relief, and Catholic Rural Life at send-off of carload of food donated from several counties in Wisconsin. 1949

Pressebild D.C.V., Frankfurt a. Main

German Church Officials receive CROP Friendship Food Ship with food from Nebraska CROP. 1948

CWS/CROP Archives

In recognition of CROP's work in Europe, John Metzler, Sr., receives from officials of West Germany a glass vase on which the activities of CROP are symbolically depicted.
c. 1950

"And who is my neighbor? . . . The one who showed him mercy." Jesus said to him, "Go and do likewise."

Luke 10:29 and 37 NRSV

If we are to do God's work, we must do it well.

J Richard Butler
Former Director of CWS

Part Two
1957–1966

As Church World Service began its second decade, it was clear that the demands being placed upon it were not tapering off. Because of both natural disasters and disasters caused by human actions, two of the biggest problems facing the world were how to feed one billion hungry people and what to do with an ever increasing number of refugees.

The face of the world was changing politically also. The French had been defeated at Dien Bien Phu and had withdrawn from Vietnam. Soviet tanks had rolled into Budapest and crushed the Hungarian uprising. Former colonies like Sudan, Ghana, and Malaysia had become independent. More than twenty other new nations declared their independence before the end of the decade. President Dwight D. Eisenhower, who had hailed the passage of the Refugee Relief Act calling it "a significant humanitarian act," had been elected to a second term.

However, as positive as some aspects of that legislation were, there were provisions of the Act, and particularly of the Amendments, which caused serious reservations among many American church members.[1] There was a continuing question about whether the churches should assume such heavy responsibilities and the guarantees that were required, or whether the government itself should be the responsible body. Among the most difficult of the requirements of the Law was called an Assurance. Such an Assurance had to show that the refugee would be suitably employed at a specific job without displacing some other person from employment, and that he or she would have specifically designated housing upon arrival in the United States. Assurances were acceptable only if they were submitted by a responsible individual citizen. The so-called "Blanket Assurances" used under the Displaced Persons Act were no longer acceptable.

Those requirements placed a heavy burden on Church World Service and its member churches. However, the commitment of CWS and the churches was so strong that in 1957, of the 61,186 refugees referred to CWS under the Refugee Relief Act, only forty-six did not receive Assurances from the American churches.[2]

Nevertheless, it was not just "refugees" from overseas who were in need of assistance. In the United States, five clergy had been forced to resign their positions because of their stand in opposition to segregation. The National Council of Churches Governing Board authorized Church World Service to come to the aid of those "political refugees in our own country." The Board also urged CWS, "to explore the possibility of instituting and financing a program of relief for ministers and their people, white or Negro, who are victims as a result of their efforts on behalf of racial justice."[3]

I

By 1957, Church World Service had resettled more than 100,000 refugees, but still the numbers waiting to be relocated continued to grow. The Hungarian Revolution had taken place the year before, and hundreds of thousands of Hungarians had fled to the West seeking freedom and a chance for a new life. The United States agreed to grant visas to some 5,000 Hungarians;

30,000 more were initially invited to come to the United States on parole, a category that includes persons admitted for humanitarian or public interest reasons. Those refugees were processed at Camp Kilmer, New Jersey, a camp run by the U.S. Army. Church World Service set up an office at the reception center at Kilmer, and staff were sent there to help process those refugees assigned to Church World Service.[4]

Nevertheless, those processing facilities were not sufficient to adequately respond to the thousands of refugees coming to the United States. So, Church World Service sent five representatives to assist the World Council of Churches (WCC) registration process in Austria. Church World Service also provided chaplains for five U.S. Navy transports that brought thousands of Hungarian refugees from Bremerhaven, Germany, to New Jersey between December 20, 1956 and February 10, 1957. Finally, CWS set up a Hungarian Protestant Chaplains' Office in Camp Kilmer to provide pastoral care and counseling, to perform marriages, and to conduct services of worship.

During 1958, Church World Service had to raise approximately $2,500,000, which had been advanced by the WCC for ocean travel loans to refugees coming to the United States, and an additional $200,000 advanced by CWS to refugees for inland transportation to their final destination. Of course, those amounts placed a severe strain on the finances of the organization.

To help meet these financial demands, Hungarian and East European refugee relief was set up as a separate item within the Church World Service budget. Ultimately, total receipts for that activity amounted to more than $45 million, including $3,442,861 in cash contributions and $34,353,315 worth of food, clothing, and material aid supplies, of which two-thirds came from the U.S. government.[5]

******

Refugee issues continued to dominate the CWS agenda in Asia and the Middle East. Many Chinese were still fleeing the

Communist government and entering Hong Kong. It was estimated that in a small area of that British colony where three million people lived, at least one-third were refugees, and up to 95 percent of those more than fourteen years of age suffered from tuberculosis. In that instance, CWS had to contend not only with the usual problems associated with refugee populations but also with starvation, disease, and lack of shelter.

Hong Kong CWS distributed millions of pounds of food and warm clothing. It built refugee housing (stone construction) and hostels, it provided health care, gave money for nurseries, and supported schools for refugee children. Church World Service also provided funds for denominational clinics, hospitals, welfare centers, orphanages, and homes for children with disabilities. In May 1957, when torrential rains flooded much of Hong Kong, CWS provided emergency funds, surplus clothing, and medicines to help the destitute and those made homeless by that typhoon-created disaster.

When a severe fire on Christmas 1954 destroyed a cluster of shanty hillside huts, about 50,000 people were left homeless. The Hong Kong government had to supply food—literally cooked rice by the shovelful—and found itself taking on the task of becoming the greatest landlord in the colony. In that respect, when the government decided to build housing, it had as its model the stone houses that had been built by CWS. A former director of the NCCC/CWS China Program wrote recently that what CWS did in the early days in Hong Kong was to be part of the miracle of the feeding of the five thousand, finding its efforts multipled a thousandfold.

******

In the Middle East, Palestinian refugees numbered about 900,000, of whom 200,000 were considered by the United Nations to be "economic refugees" and therefore not eligible for United Nations relief. A World Council of Churches and International Missionary Council Conference in 1956 had said that "the plight of

Palestinian refugees in the Middle East stands out in its particular misery of frustration and affronts the conscience of mankind." Yet the member nations of the United Nations appeared to care little about the Palestinian refugees, together allocating about $30 per person per year for their needs.

The churches, mainly through CWS and Lutheran World Relief, were the only source of clothing for the Palestinian refugees. In addition, CWS worked to improve housing and developed programs that provided food for children. In West Jordan, two million pounds of food were distributed, while in East Jordan there were vocational training classes, as well as food and clothing distribution programs.

The attention of the world, meanwhile, was on the Suez crisis. In October 1956, Britain and France had joined Israel in the bombardment of Egyptian lines, rendering another 100,000 Arabs homeless.[6] Again it was the churches who made a significant response. Churches from the United States, Great Britain, and France sent more than $40,000 in cash and thousands of pounds of food, clothing, medicines, and cooking utensils to the area. In doing so, the ability of the churches to respond quickly again was proved as they drew upon reserves and reassigned shipments to meet overwhelming human need.

While the refugee crisis in the Middle East continued to grow, refugees were also fleeing Chinese troops that had moved into Tibet. More than 40,000 refugees crossed the mountainous border from Tibet into India. The government of India did as much as possible, but the numbers continued to increase rapidly. By 1959 the number of refugees in and around Calcutta had grown to more than three million. Some were housed in massed camps, thousands more slept on the streets, on sidewalks and in railway stations. Church World Service, with representatives of the WCC and the YMCA, brought emergency supplies, food, clothing, and medicines, in an attempt to relieve what some experienced observers thought was the most tragic human refugee situation in the world.

******

That same year also saw CWS become involved in Burma and again in Indonesia. In Burma, war and natural disasters had created more than 50,000 refugees; Rangoon alone had 75,000 homeless. Church World Service responded by supplying food, supporting a rural training program, and aiding a hospital operated by the Burma Christian Medical Relief Society.

A few years earlier, political disturbances had caused CWS to curtail its work in Indonesia. Nevertheless, when floods struck central and east Java, affecting 600,000 people, CWS borrowed 100,000 pounds of powdered milk from UNICEF and cabled $2,000 in funds. Through CROP it appealed for and assembled shipments of food and clothing.

There is no question but that a major focus of CWS activity in the late 1950s was Asia. A catastrophic emergency developed in Taiwan when a typhoon, an earthquake, and the worst floods in many years struck the country almost simultaneously; 250,000 people were left homeless. Taiwan Christian Service emptied its warehouses of supplies, and army planes carried them into the stricken areas. When roads were not passable or did not exist, porters carried relief supplies to remote villages on their backs. Multivitamins were airlifted from the United States and emergency funds were sent by CWS from New York.

******

Nineteen fifty-nine was a year of both good news and bad news. Japan had become a source of particular satisfaction for CWS. In the face of the global challenges it faced and the growth of Japan's indigenous leadership, CWS turned over its Japan office to leaders in the Japanese churches. That marked the beginning of a process phasing out CWS offices in some forty countries, and the beginning of a new era of partnership with indigenous churches. The Japanese church people had come to realize that Japan CWS was their own agency and that it had developed unusual skill and competence in handling disasters and other emergencies.

It could cooperate fully with the government in many situations while still maintaining its integrity as a Christian organization. Records show that Japan CWS had developed such significant local support from Japanese churches and the public that it required little ongoing budget support from the United States. However, when a tidal wave struck parts of Japan, CWS sent $32,000 from New York to help Japan CWS in recovery efforts.

That year in Africa, anti-government riots had occurred in Algeria, and the French army had seized power in that country. Many Algerian refugees from the North African battles were crowded together in several internment camps in France and CWS shipped clothing and made CROP foods available to them.

In North Africa itself, almost two million Algerians had been left homeless by the war for independence. Many had fled their villages that had been destroyed, and 1.5 million people were living in "regrouping centers," over one-half of them children.

Protestant and Catholic churches united in a worldwide appeal for funds, clothing, medicines, and food for the Algerians. Church World Service responded to the appeal with an initial $10,000 in cash, along with vitamins, clothing, blankets, sugar, and corn oil. CROP assisted in raising many of those emergency supplies and funds.

Another demand upon CWS staff and resources in 1959 was Greece. Although international help had benefited many in that country, the poorest third of the people had not been helped. Many lived on the incredibly low income of $32 a year.[7] At the time, CWS had a staff of twenty-seven in Greece, but during the year that small staff helped more than 2.5 million people with food and other relief supplies.

Programs were being carried out in Poland, Portugal, Turkey, and Yugoslavia at the same time. Working with Lutheran World Relief and the Yugoslav Red Cross, Church World Service helped provide school lunches, including milk, for two million children, resulting in a significant drop in the tuberculosis rate among children.

The Arab refugee situation was not improving. The population of the camps in and around Palestine had by now reached one million, with little prospect for improvement in sight. Protestant agencies were the only source of clothing, and during that year CWS provided clothing for 600,000 refugees. It also gave $300,000 to support the Near East Christian Council Committee for Refugee Work (NECCCRW). Those funds were used for poultry projects, agricultural assistance, loans, and medical care. By the end of the tumultuous year of 1959, Church World Service was active in fifty countries around the world.

Recognizing the increasing number of refugees worldwide, the General Assembly of the United Nations adopted a resolution through which the "World Refugee Year" was created. For twelve months, beginning June 1, 1959, attention was to focus on "the refugee problem and to encourage additional financial contributions from governments, voluntary agencies and the public." The resolution also hoped to encourage additional opportunities for permanent refugee solutions on a "purely humanitarian basis."

The Food and Agriculture Organization of the United Nations (FAO) launched a five-year Freedom-From-Hunger campaign in 1960 and designated 1963 as "World Hunger Year." Through these two programs, the United Nations attempted to focus the attention of the nations of the world on the two major problems facing humanity at the beginning of the 1960s: refugees and world hunger.

II

Closer to home, problems existed in Latin America and the Caribbean. A serious drought in the northeast corner of Brazil had resulted in great human need. With Lutheran World Relief, CWS began feeding programs to serve the hungry in Brazil and other places in Latin America. Dwight Swartzendruber, director of the CWS Latin America Office, in cooperation with the WCC and church officials in Brazil, helped create Diaconia, an organization designed to initiate and support church-related economic development programs. Church World Service and Lutheran World Relief together supported a feeding program in Chile, which initially served only 25,000, but in time was expanded to include 125,000. The CWS counterpart organization in Chile, Ayuda Cristiana Evangelica, eventually had more than 400 local distribution committees to select and vouch for recipients and to account for every pound of food received.[8]

However, it was the situation in Cuba, in the Caribbean, that eventually would have the greatest long-term impact on CWS. President Fulgencio Batista had been overthrown, and Fidel Castro had become Prime Minister. The political situation, compounded by serious floods, caused many Cubans to cluster in Oriente province where more than 50,000 were hungry and homeless. The Cuban Federation of Churches appealed to CWS for help. Besides providing $5,000 cash, arrangements were made for a U.S. Navy reserve unit to airlift food (supplied by CROP), multivitamins, and clothing to the island. Ocean shipments were also made, but because of political considerations, freight reimbursement funds were not available from the United States. The shipments made to Cuba that year cost CWS $62,000 for ocean freight alone.

When the nature and intent of the Castro government became known, tens of thousands of Cuban refugees left the country. Many of them headed for Miami. The United States had become a country of first asylum. In the past, most refugees coming to the United States had passed through a third country. This was the first time the United States began to experience what many other countries had experienced—large numbers of refugees uninvited and unexpected. Miami in particular began to have serious social and economic problems.

Most of the Cubans who had come to the United States thought that their stay would be short and that Castro would soon be overthrown. But the Bay of Pigs in 1961 changed all that. It was clear they probably could not return to their homeland. Church World Service had opened a Miami office to provide services to the refugees, but the problem of finding enough sponsors in the Miami area was overwhelming. Extraordinary steps evidently had to be taken.

James MacCracken, director of CWS immigration services, and later executive director of CWS, organized a series of "Flights for Freedom." He arranged for block bookings on airlines to certain cities, where councils of churches agreed to find individuals or congregations willing to serve as sponsors for the Cubans. A CWS staff person from New York or Miami would greet the flights as they arrived and coordinate the resettlement process.[9]

Between February 1962 and October 1963, there were sixty-three flights to thirty-five cities in twenty-two states. One such Church World Service flight, which required more than one plane, took 118 persons to Kansas City, while another carried ninety to Denver. Both regularly scheduled airlines and charter airlines were used depending on the number of refugees on a particular flight. Some repeat flights were necessary to various cities as friends or relatives joined those who had gone before. In all, 3,692 persons were resettled using those "Flights for Freedom."

In 1961, Church World Service sponsored a "Consultation on Immigration Policy in the United States" in Washington. The consultation brought together not only church leaders, but also U.S. government officials including Chester Bowles, Under Secretary of State and Senator Kenneth Keating of New York. The purpose of the consultation was to review the United States record in refugee resettlement and to reflect on the total idea of population movements in the world today—a question that would be very important in the years ahead. The results of that consultation found their way into the presidential message John F. Kennedy sent to Congress on July 23, 1963, recommending a new formula governing immigration into the United States.

As important as resettlement was for many refugees, it was impossible for many others. At the same time, even when it became possible for some people to return to their homeland, it was often very difficult to start life over. When refugees returned to Algeria, they found many of their orchards and wooded areas burned away; their way of life had been destroyed by the war. In response to that tragic situation, CWS supported a WCC consortium, the Christian Committee for Service in Algeria (CCSA). From 1962 to 1966, CCSA was directed by Hans L. Aurbakken, a missionary in Algeria since 1936 and the father of Mia Adjali, a member of the present CWS Board of Directors. Using CROP commodities, and later U.S. government surplus commodities, CWS developed "Food-for-Work" projects, a system that had been used in India with considerable success. Food was used as wages so that both the people and the communities benefited. Several thousand workers were used to terrace hillsides and to plant more than 27 million fruit, olive, and other kinds of trees. That reforestation program provided lumber, but also helped to control soil erosion and surface water in eastern Algeria. Eventually, many people trained in that project became key personnel in the Algerian Department of Forestry.[10]

In was not just in Algeria that Church World Service programs resulted in new African leadership. The Ecumenical Scholarship Fund that CWS supported for many years resulted in four persons who had benefited from that program being appointed as cabinet ministers in the government of Southern Sudan.[11]

******

It was during these years that several individuals joined the staff of CWS and were to play significant roles in the evolution of CWS as an organization.

In 1962, J Richard Butler, a future executive director of Church World Service, became executive secretary of the Near East Council of Churches Committee on Refugee Work. He had come to the Middle East two years earlier, secunded to CWS by the Congregational Christian Service Committee. From the very beginning of his tenure, Dick Butler adopted two themes: flexibility and excellence. He tightened administrative procedures, moved the staff to higher professional standards, encouraged greater coordination among the various players, and urged committees to undergo thorough self-examination evaluations. He is reported to have said in his first report, "If we are to do God's work, we must do it well."[12] All these qualities were to be evident in his future role as executive director of CWS during difficult times.

In those same years, Franklin Woo, later director of the NCCC/CWS China Program, began working in Hong Kong. Secunded to CWS by the United Presbyterians, Woo was assigned to the Student Christian Center where more than 400 refugee students from six colleges worked in more than 100 projects throughout the colony. Some worked at food distribution among the refugees, in milk stations, or put in ten hours a week either as tutor or teacher in the "rooftop schools" for refugee children in the resettlement areas.

By that time, the Marshall Plan had helped Europe recover from the devastation of World War II, the Cold War had set in, and western Kansas was in its seventh year of severe drought. It was in those days that Lowell Brown, an Evangelical United Brethren pastor in western Kansas, was asked to join the staff of CROP. Having served successfully as local campaign director in the county seat, he was urged to come on staff full-time. In the next thirty years the names CROP and Lowell Brown became almost synonymous. Brown became an assistant director in Kansas, regional director in Illinois, and eventually director of the office of Community Outreach for the entire CROP regional office network. Brown completed his work with CWS as special assistant to the executive director of CWS.

Again, the stories of committed Christian individuals like Dick Butler, Franklin Woo, and Lowell Brown are the stories behind the story of CWS.

III

The early to mid-1960s were busy years for Church World Service. During 1964, CWS helped more than six million people in forty countries.[13] Including commodities supplied by the U.S. government, that year it shipped 387,393,000 pounds of food, clothing, and medical supplies valued at $32,952,416. That was also the year when the long-awaited and important debate was held on the role of churches in the use of government commodities. The questions that had been raised when PL 480 was passed ten years before had never been fully resolved.

Church World Service had appointed a committee of staff people from CWS and the NCCC Division of Foreign Missions to study the issue. The committee sought input from 300 missionaries, local pastors in countries receiving goods, ecumenical leaders, and CWS staff overseas. The committee's recommendations were extensive. Eventually, after much debate, they were accepted by the General Board of the NCCC.

The key recommendation was that CWS should continue the distribution overseas of PL 480 commodities and that their use did not "jeopardize the historic position of the American churches concerning the separation of church and state, when accompanied by appropriate safeguards." The committee also recommended that CWS should encourage "indigenous agencies in the countries in which it was attempting to serve to assume additional responsibility . . . and be prepared to relinquish control to them as soon as they were able to carry on its responsibilities." This latter recommendation was precisely what had been the operational philosophy of CWS and practice for many years.

Church World Service continued to respond to disasters and emergencies wherever they struck. There were twenty-three such responses called for in 1964. Church World Service had been in business long enough to have acquired some experience and expertise in disaster response. It knew where disasters were likely to strike and kept resources available in strategic places—New Windsor, Maryland; Houston, Texas; and Modesto, California. When disasters occurred, the necessary supplies were ready to go immediately, often by air freight.

In the early 1960s, India began to suffer one of the worst extended droughts in its history. Some areas of the subcontinent had total monsoon failure for three years, resulting in major crop failure. In some provinces there were no crops and no water for human consumption. People literally died of thirst as streams dried up and wells went dry. The drought would go on for years, with Church World Service working to respond through the Committee on Relief and Gift Supplies (CORAGS), the National Christian Council of India's relief operation.

In the midst of the drought, the already overburdened resources of India were overwhelmed when another 100,000 refugees from East Pakistan crossed over into Assam and West Bengal. In response to an appeal from the churches of India, CWS immediately sent $5,000 in cash, and the WCC raised another $60,000. By the end of the year, there were more than 275,000 victims of the Hindu/Moslem conflicts in ninety-seven camps. To further complicate an already difficult situation, while India was attempting to feed and shelter refugees from East Pakistan, East Pakistan itself received 350,000 Muslims who had been driven out of India. PL 480 foods and CWS clothing were sent to both places to meet the needs of those thousands crossing the border in both directions.

Famine in Java, a volcanic eruption on the island of Bali, an earthquake in Japan, and floods in Korea caused CWS reserves to be drawn upon heavily. Korea in particular was the scene of recurring disasters, and more than thirty-three million pounds of CWS material aid were sent to Korea in 1964 alone.

Africa was also the recipient of large amounts—approximately 50,000 tons—of CWS aid in 1964. The largest portions went to war-stricken Algeria with the second largest going to the Congo. Besides the Congo's own internal problems, 75,000 homeless

Angolans had crossed over into that country, and CWS began an emergency feeding program for 21,000 of those uprooted people. It also distributed seeds and tools for agricultural projects, to enable them to become more self-sufficient.

However, the biggest task of disaster relief during 1964 took place in Haiti. That island nation had been struck by the most severe Caribbean hurricane of the century. Church World Service sponsored Food-for-Work projects, providing employment for thousands working on road building, the development of water or irrigation systems, and the building of schools. In the aftermath of the hurricane, CWS food was distributed to 170 schools or canteens for youth, and served about 15,000 children.

******

One of the most demanding tasks facing CWS was the selection of staff for the overseas offices of what had become a global organization. The principle that CWS followed was that it should have as few western foreign personnel as possible in its overseas operations. That meant that each program generally relied on one key staff person, or in some larger programs, the minimum number necessary. The selection of those staff persons was crucial to the functions of CWS, for it meant not only program administration but also training local people to take over the carrying out and direction of the programs as soon as possible.

IV

It had been almost ten years since Church World Service was first involved in Vietnam. Yet as hostilities in that country increased in 1964, CWS again began working in Vietnam in cooperation with the Mennonite Central Committee (MCC), which already had a relief operation headquartered in Saigon. When a flood struck South Vietnam, killing several thousand people and making many more homeless, CWS sent aid through the MCC. Those supplies were airlifted to Vietnam through an arrangement with the U.S. Agency for International Development (USAID) in Washington. In addition, CWS-Hong Kong forwarded 350,000 pounds of flour and 79,000 pounds of CROP soybeans and other commodities to that country.

However, as the U.S. military presence grew, as the war disrupted the lives of millions of Vietnamese, as refugees streamed south fleeing from North Vietnam, and as Americans focused their attention on this previously little known country, the churches began to raise questions about their possible role in Vietnam. J. Harry Haines, a member of the CWS Department Committee, who had been the first Church World Service Southeast area director in 1952, traveled extensively in South Vietnam to determine the conditions in that country and what, if anything, the churches should be doing.

Protestant church members across the United States were asking what they could do to help relieve human suffering among the more than 69,000 refugees camping in various provinces of South Vietnam. Christians made up only a tiny minority in Vietnam, and as a result of the French colonial background that heavily favored Roman Catholic missions, there were few Protestants. Nevertheless, the desire to provide assistance remained strong among Protestant church people in the United States.

One response to that desire was the creation, by Church World Service, Lutheran World Relief, and the Mennonite Central Committee, of a separate organization to be called Vietnam Christian Service (VNCS). The focus of the agency was to be refugees, a "Christian Presence" in the midst of sorrow and suffering "which would provide healing, counseling, teaching and other services."[14]

By late 1965, the year VNCS was created, it included a medical program in one province and a countrywide material aid operation that distributed food and clothing to 215,000 refugees, Montagnards, and other needy. By early 1966, community development projects were starting and a clinic at Pleiku was being built.

Initially, the staff of VNCS consisted of nine from the MCC, one CWS worker, one Brethren Service Commission volunteer, and several Vietnamese. In the middle of 1966, the number of overseas staff had increased to twenty-nine. By the time VNCS was ended nine years later, it had included approximately 200 Vietnamese and 200 overseas staff, and it had used resources in excess of $10,300,000.[15] During 1965, CWS had also sent four nurses to Vietnam to work with Mennonite Central Committee staff to care for refugees and victims of typhoons that had ravaged that country earlier in the year.

V

Organizationally, significant changes affecting CWS were again taking place. Conversations had been underway for some time within the National Council of Churches about the need to reduce overlapping activities in its various divisions. By 1965, the decision had been made to reorganize the council. As part of that reorganization, the Division of Foreign Missions (DFM) and Church World Service were brought together and the Division of Overseas Ministries (DOM) was created. In essence, the DOM was the former DFM with CWS now a department within the new division. Each of the geographical area offices (Latin America, Africa, Asia, the Middle East and Europe) was administered by former DFM personnel with a CWS area director as part of the team. The CWS role was to respond to disasters, to oversee all service programs of the DOM, and to supervise development projects that CWS had begun in the various geographic areas.

Besides the geographic area offices through which the increasingly important overseas economic and social development programs and projects were undertaken, CWS continued to have departments dealing with material aid services (including CROP), refugee and immigration services, promotional services, and administration.

James MacCracken, who had been director of the CWS

Immigration and Refugee Program, became Executive Director of Church World Service. Church World Service also continued to be a legal corporation (CWS, Inc.) registered with the U.S. government and other governments as an agency for receiving ocean freight reimbursement and PL 480 surplus foods. In the reorganization, it was also made clear that funds given to CWS by the denominations and received from public appeals were to be used strictly for CWS programs and projects. The intent of the donor was to be fulfilled as a matter of organizational integrity.

Nineteen sixty-five was the year that CWS had its first staff person die in the line of duty. Theodore Kimmel had been assigned to Madagascar as an advisor to the Protestant Social Welfare Service. Killed in an airplane accident at age 36, he left behind a wife and three daughters. The crash, which also killed an American businessman and a French government official, had occurred in a remote area. It was several days before news of the accident reached CWS. Shortly before his death, Ted Kimmel had written an extensive article for the CROP Service News in which he praised the use of CROP foods in development projects and school-feeding programs in Madagascar, but went on to say, "We must not be content with just handing out food. Our real job is teaching and inspiring."[16]

Meanwhile, changes were also taking place in CROP. The CWS Clothing Program, which had been part of the CWS Material Resources Program since 1946, had become the responsibility of CROP and the Elkhart office. As early as 1945, American church women had responded to an appeal from war-torn Europe for clothing, towels, and bedding. By 1950, contributions of clothing came in such large amounts that processing and shipping costs, which were not provided by the donors, were placing a serious strain on the finances of CWS. That problem was lessened when a decision was made to request that donors contribute ten cents a pound to help in the processing of their gifts.

By the late 1960s, the Clothing Program became a major factor in providing support for worldwide relief and development activities of Church World Service. Under the supervision of Lila McCray, and operating through CROP regional offices, CWS was soon receiving four million pounds of washable, durable clothing and 300,000 blankets a year. Layettes, health kits, and school kits were added to the items requested and church women's groups throughout the country participated in the clothing program. Trucks from the Brethren Service Center made scheduled visits to collection points around the United States and delivered the clothing, kits, and blankets to New Windsor, Maryland for processing and shipping. CROP also provided instructions so that church groups could sew items that were particularly needed in overseas programs. To enlarge the program, Church Women United donated eight sewing machines to be used in the New Windsor Clothing Center for sewing cut garment sets and layettes. Besides regular shipments, clothing and blankets were baled and stored in a warehouse for immediate airlifting in case of an emergency.

CROP also arranged with various companies for contributions of their products. Elvin Frantz worked out a plan with the Ferry-Morse Seed company for the discount purchase of new seeds in aluminum packets to guarantee germination after overseas shipping. The seed packets, along with other commodities from food producers, often added up to $2 million worth of contributions from corporations each year. The Sperry and Hutchinson Company, the "Green Stamp" people, redeemed thousands of S&H Green Stamp booklets sent to CROP by women throughout the United States. The cash received was used to purchase blankets for CWS to ship to needy areas overseas.

With the addition of the Clothing Program, CROP began to extend its activities into urban areas. Ralph Taylor, one of the senior CROP staff, was made responsible for introducing CROP to churches and communities on the East Coast. His "region" stretched from Maine to below the nation's capital. CROP was no longer just a "rural" commodity collection program. To reflect that change, and to help appeal to all segments of the American public, the name was changed to Church World Service Community

Appeals. CROP became the "trademark" of CWS public appeals. No longer was CROP an acronym.

Many state programs were established through state councils of churches. Occasionally, the state council incorporated the CROP program into its own structure, in other cases it merely sponsored and endorsed CROP as an independent agency. In the first instance the state council hired the local director with national CROP approval. In the second model it was just the opposite, with national CROP hiring the regional director with the knowledge and approval of the state council. Of course, those dual arrangements, including the appropriate roles of the local CROP committee and the national CROP Committee, presented some challenging personnel and financial issues.

The evolution of CROP in places like Ohio and Michigan are case histories of how the organization and its program changed over the years. Beginning as rural commodity collection programs, they became not only outstanding income-producing states for CWS, but also regions with strong educational programs about the root causes of hunger and poverty in the world.

VI

The great India drought that had begun in 1963 continued to cause hunger, malnutrition, and suffering throughout the country. Over the years, church relief agencies had stepped up their aid to the stricken country, but the aid provided by the churches was not sufficient. In March 1966, representatives of the National Christian Council of India and the Roman Catholic Church brought together representatives of churches, foundations, agencies, and governments to figure out what more could be done. Participating in the conference besides the churches were representatives from the Ford and Rockefeller Foundations and USAID. Out of that three-day session came a coordinating and planning organization given the name of Action for Food Production (AFPRO).

Appeals issued by AFPRO were responded to immediately by the churches of the world. Millions of dollars were provided for the purchase of seed, fertilizer, tractors, and credit to help small farmers to produce more food. Expansion of water resources and the digging of wells became a priority. Irrigation pumps and well-drilling equipment were purchased. Thousands of Food-for-Work projects were undertaken employing tens of thousands of men and women and supported financially by CWS.

******

As Church World Service celebrated its twentieth anniversary in 1966, besides the increasingly important work in long-term development, it continued to respond to emergencies worldwide on behalf of the NCCC and its member communions. Emergency calls on CWS resulted in 90,000 pounds of clothing for the victims of disastrous earthquakes in Turkey and Greece. It sent food and other emergency supplies to Southern Haiti, where the fury of Hurricane Inez had destroyed half the buildings and left hundreds dead or injured. CROP airlifted 90,000 packets of vegetable seeds and sent 200,000 pounds of grain and powdered milk and building supplies to that country by ship. At the same time, CROP reported encouraging response to its appeals for flood-stricken Korea and East Pakistan, and for war-devastated Vietnam.

As the second decade in the life of CWS and CROP came to a close, Albert Farmer wrote,

> Since 1959 an increasing share of CROP gifts have been used for assisting agricultural development. In that year CROP foods were first used to pay wages for building a farm-to-market road, pioneering in what is known as 'Food-for-Work' in which large amounts of foods are now used. For the past three years, more than half of all CROP shipments have been used for community development, either as seeds and equipment or as 'Food-for-Work.'"[17] Integrated rural development programs using CROP foods and other agricultural supplies and equipment had become a major CWS activity.

A child is examined at a maternal and child health clinic in India, funded through CWS. 1965

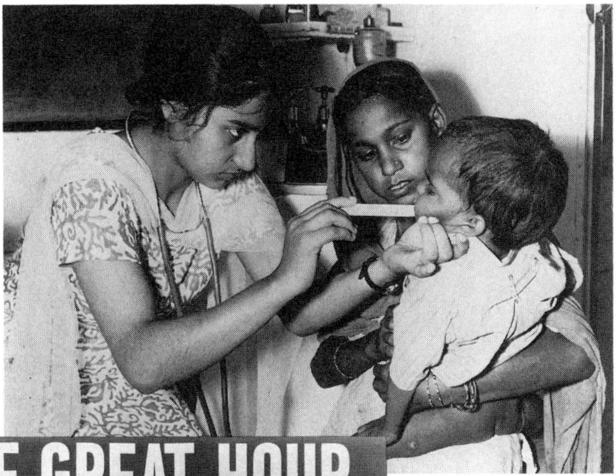

CWS/CROP Archives

CWS/CROP Archives

ONE GREAT HOUR
OF
SHARING
CHURCH WORLD SERVICE
National Council of the Churches of Christ in the U.S.A.
475 Riverside Drive
New York 27, N.Y.

An early One Great Hour of Sharing poster designed to raise funds for Church World Service. 1962

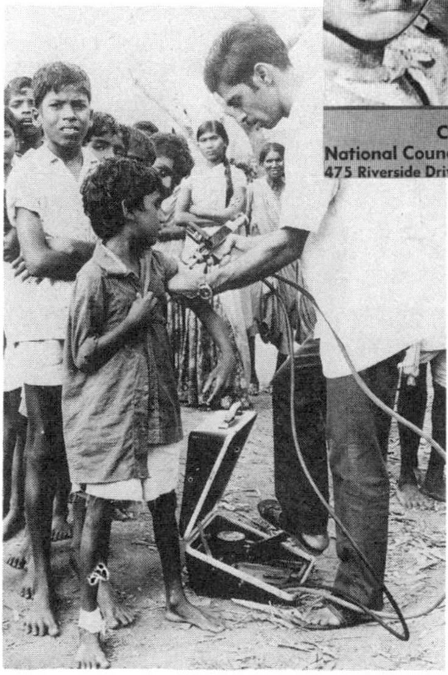

CASA/CWS

A Church's Auxiliary for Social Action (CASA) worker inoculating children in a cyclone-stricken region of India. CASA is a long-time CWS partner agency. 1977

CWS/CROP Archives

Planting trees: A CWS/CROP
Food-for-Work project in Algeria following the
Algerian war of independence. 1965

WE SHARE IN
FRIENDSHIP
ACRES
A CROP PROJECT

CWS/CROP Archives

A farmer who set aside an acre of his farm and contributed its produce
to CROP. 1961

Is not this the fast that I choose: to loose the bonds of injustice . . . to let the oppressed go free . . . and to break every yoke? Is it not to share your bread with the hungry, and bring the homeless poor into your house . . .

Isaiah 58:6–7 NRSV

Injustice anywhere is a threat to justice everywhere.

Dr. Martin Luther King, Jr.

Part Three

1967–1976

The mid to late sixties were tumultuous years nationally and internationally, and by all accounts busy times for Church World Service.

Internationally, the United States had become more deeply involved in Vietnam, with the landing of thousands of additional U.S. troops and the bombing of North Vietnamese bases. Fighting was continuing between Greeks and Turks on Cyprus, and India had invaded West Pakistan. Following a military coup in Nigeria, the province of Biafra had declared its independence, leading to a civil war and the deaths of one million people. In the Middle East, there was the Six-Day War between Israel and Arab states, and in Teheran the Shah of Iran had been crowned. The *U.S. Pueblo* had been seized by North Korea, and martial law was declared throughout Vietnam.

During those years, the United States was recovering from the assassination of President John F. Kennedy, and President Lyndon Johnson signed into law the Civil Rights Act of 1964. Antiwar demonstrations had begun on the campuses and in the streets protesting the country's involvement in Vietnam. Before the decade was over, four student demonstrators had been killed by National Guard troops at Kent State University in Ohio. Within a period of six weeks in 1968, Martin Luther King, Jr., and Robert Kennedy had been assassinated, and a sitting president, Lyndon Johnson, had decided, in the face of antiwar demonstrations and civil unrest, not to run for reelection. Violent riots occurred during that year's Democratic Party Convention in Chicago, and later that year Richard Nixon was elected president of the United States.

I

The 1960s saw both natural disasters and disasters caused by human actions claim the lives of millions of people. An earthquake in Iran killed 20,000, while a drought began in Africa that would cause the loss of a million head of cattle and thousands of human lives.

The onset of that drought emergency came as no surprise to Church World Service. A concern had been growing within the agency for some time that a world famine of unprecedented proportions was impending, and that plans should be made immediately to avert, or at least, prepare for that crisis. A paper, "World Hunger and American Christian Responsibility," was prepared by CWS in March 1965, and presented to the Division of Overseas Ministries. Based on that paper, within a few months, the National Council of Churches adopted a resolution urging the U.S. government to initiate actions designed to make freedom from hunger a reality.[1]

That predicted famine became a reality when, in a wide band across Africa, in the Sahel, south of the Sahara desert, almost no rain fell for six years (1968 to 1974) exposing 23 million people in six countries to the threat of annihilation.[2] Most of the people were rural and nomadic, their existence being sustained in large part by constant movement to avoid putting strain on sparse vegetation. The people of the Sahel eked out a meager existence in the best of times. Moving from one grazing area to another, trading with more sedentary people, they lived on the very edge of survival. When the drought came, it was clear that thousands would evidently not survive without outside help.

Once the extent of the disaster was known, an international task force was created to deliver much needed help to that area. Under colonial rule, little had been done to develop infrastructures of communication and transportation; those roads that did exist were completely inadequate to handle the distribution of relief supplies. Aid for the most part had to be delivered by air drops.

Church World Service's initial involvement in the Sahel was in supporting feeding programs, mostly in Mali and Niger. It also contributed to a World Council of Churches consortium working in Upper Volta and Mauritania. Nevertheless, it was after the immediate emergency was over, that CWS undertook its most important work in the Sahel—that of rehabilitation.

The Sahel experience was a sobering reminder of humanity's reliance on the health of the ecosystem in the world in which we live. The crucial role of nature in the survival of people and cultures can never be overestimated. The introduction of advanced and sometimes inappropriate technology often adds to the problems of an area, rather than diminishing them. The danger of that happening in the Sahel was evident as large amounts of aid and assistance poured in, often with disastrous results. The Sahel was a lesson in the kinds of development activities that often add to the problems faced by the people of a stricken area. Church World Service tried to avoid that possibility by using technology and activities appropriate to local people and their environment.

In Niger, CWS had been active since the mid-1950s. Its activities had included dunes control, helping develop school vegetable gardens, irrigation systems, the stocking of lakes, and the planting of date palms. Dates were a basic part of the diet of that country. People depended heavily upon them for much needed food. However, like the biblical plagues that followed one upon another, when the drought was over, an insect appeared covering the leaves of the date palms with a waxy scale that destroyed the trees. The one defense against the insects was ladybugs that kept them in check.

In an attempt to save the date palms, cuttings were taken to other oases for replanting. Yet while the damaging insects survived the move, the ladybugs did not, so a different kind of ladybug was needed if the date palms were to survive. Through experimentation, it was found that a species of ladybugs found in Iran was especially effective against scale-producing insects. Church World Service financed the sending of thousands of those Iranian ladybugs to Niger.

Elsewhere, CWS supported a variety of other projects designed to help people cope with the drought and its aftermath. Nevertheless, the Sahel had made it clear that the work of voluntary organizations was not sufficient in face of such overwhelming need. There needed to be a more alert international community ready to move into areas stricken by such disasters, and much more needed to be learned about what kind of development activities were appropriate in such situations. The Sahel experience showed the enormous complexity of the development process, and how making serious mistakes is easy even with the best of intentions.

The United Nations had declared the 1960s as the Decade of Development. Still, at the time, probably few, if any, understood what authentic development was all about. There were many theories, but little agreement. What did happen was that the debate concerning the relative merits of relief and development was intensified. Church groups were involved in that debate; differences of opinion between service-oriented people and mission people were strong and ongoing.

In Africa, in the late sixties another major disaster was evolving, one that would take one million lives before it was resolved. This one, unlike the Sahel, was the result of human actions. In 1966, two military coups had occurred in Nigeria, six months apart. The following year, the eastern region of the country, Biafra, declared its independence, thrusting the country into civil war.

One aspect of the relief vs. development debate was whether or not providing relief to hungry and suffering people did in fact strengthen an oppressive government by keeping people more servile. Nigeria and its breakaway region of Biafra were a case in point. When the government of Nigeria blockaded Biafra, the World Council of Churches appealed for aid for civilian victims on both sides, then turned the relief operation over to a Joint Church Aid (JCA) operation in which CWS and Catholic Relief Services (CRS) were the principal players.

The JCA secured four C97 freightliners from the United States and formed an "air bridge" to Biafra. By the end of 1969, 5,000 flights had carried 50,000 tons of supplies to an airstrip that was nothing more than a reinforced blacktop road. Three air crews lost their lives in that operation. When it was suggested by some in the churches, including the WCC, that the flights be ceased for political reasons, CWS representatives told the leaders of the Division of Overseas Ministries that the result of the abolition of the airlift would mean death to untold numbers of people.

In summing up the CWS position, Jim MacCracken wrote, "Many may have sincerely felt that the flights were prolonging the agony of the people of Nigeria: this is probably so, I don't have the data on that. At the end of the conflict one thing was clear: the children of Biafra were alive."[3] The Biafra experience made it obvious that providing relief in such situations did have political implications, but to have withheld relief aid would also have had political implications.

II

Meanwhile, CWS was active on other fronts. One of the largest food programs in Asia was in the Ryukyu Islands, jointly sponsored and administered by CWS and Catholic Relief

Services. Although there had been a disagreement between the U.N. High Commissioner and the voluntary agencies over control of the program, in part because it involved the use of PL 480 commodities, the program reached about 500,000 children annually. Besides the government surplus commodities, the use of CROP foods added a flexible and creative element to the programming. According to Gary Ambrose, the CWS representative who went out to the Ryukyu Islands in 1967, CROP supplies allowed the program to help the rural poor with tools, seeds, and fertilizer—an element that could not be accomplished through PL 480.

According to Ambrose, the fact that the program had been developed jointly by CWS and CRS, and then successfully turned over to the local government was a worthwhile and noteworthy accomplishment. It showed again that CWS did not plan to stay in countries that could and would handle their own challenges. In his report on that program, Ambrose wrote, "There is a time to help and there is a time to transfer programs when local entities are willing and able to take care of their own."[4] That had long been an operating principle of Church World Service.

Also in Asia, the activities of Vietnam Christian Service (VNCS) had become quite varied by 1967. In several different parts of the country, VNCS personnel had undertaken refugee feeding programs. They were helping in elementary and secondary education, as well as vocational education activities, literacy programs, health clinics, and home economic classes to mention but a few ways VNCS staff were becoming involved in Vietnam.

By 1968, the VNCS sponsoring agencies—CWS, Lutheran World Relief, and Mennonite Central Committee—were holding a series of discussions concerning, "Post-Hostilities Christian Service in Vietnam."[5] A memo to the CWS Department Committee emphasized the importance of remaining open to the changing situation in Vietnam, the need to avoid rigid politically-defined policy, and questioned the assumption that the emergency response was temporary. It was believed that the needs in Vietnam after the cessation of hostilities would be so massive that a very special refugee and community development organization would probably be required to deal with those many problems. The involvement of U.S. churches in Vietnam was clearly not to be a short-term effort. One personal tragedy associated with VNCS was the death of Ted Studebaker, a CWS staff person from the Church of the Brethren, killed by gunfire in April 1971.

Civil unrest had broken out in the Philippines, resulting in the deaths of hundreds of persons and making refugees of thousands. In June and July of 1971, hundreds of refugees started arriving in Marawi City from outlying rural areas, driven from their homes by the fighting between Bangsa Moro Army units and government forces. Lloyd Van Vactor, a member of the United Church of Christ and then president of Dansalan College in the Philippines, remembers being assured by Kirk Alliman, the CWS representative, that CWS would provide basic food stuffs for refugees living in the city.

The major relief agencies in the Philippines at the time—Catholic Relief Services, Church World Service, and the Seventh Day Adventist World Service—agreed among themselves to divide the troubled region of Mindanao into three sections for their involvement and support. Church World Service was the agency that responded to the needs of the Lanao province.

A Muslim-Christian Brotherhood was organized by concerned Muslims and Christians to help in the relief efforts. That organization took responsibility for the distribution of supplies as they arrived in the area. Lloyd Van Vactor remembers that besides food, there were also blankets and clothing shipped by CWS in Manila. Major food distribution continued for several months until the number of refugees was reduced—when refugees could return to their homes or were able to find means of self-support within Marawi City. After the food distribution was ended, at the suggestion of CWS and USAID, thousands of "Nutri-buns" were sent to school children in Marawi City. Based on a recipe sent by CWS, and using flour and milk supplied by USAID, a local bakery made the buns that were made available to children for several months until the need lessened.

III

Changes were also underway in CROP. As we have seen, by the mid-1960s CROP was no longer just a rural commodity collection program. Its appeal was now to all segments of the American public, and to reflect that change, its name had been changed to the Church World Service Community Appeal. Since 1947, CROP had been part of the CWS Material Aid Department. However, in 1969, it became an independent unit of CWS, and officials from Elkhart became part of the CWS management team, participating in weekly strategy and planning sessions in New York.

Nevertheless, CROP had not abandoned its rural roots nor forgotten the contributions made by U.S. farmers in its early days. Many of those same farmers wanted to still play an important and active role in the organization. One way they did so was to create a program known as "Friendship Acres." Originated by an Indiana farmer, Marvin Mishler, "Friendship Acres" were modeled on the "Lord's Acre" idea in which individual farmers set aside the produce of one acre of ground and contributed it to help hungry people through CROP. The idea of "Friendship Acres" was taken up in other regions and they became the source of considerable income for CWS/CROP in the 1960s and 1970s. A spinoff was the creation of "Friendship Farms," in which large pieces of land comprising many acres were designated to provide commodities for CROP. Those cooperative farms were seeded, cultivated, and harvested by groups of local farmers, and the produce from them resulted in additional income for CWS.

At the same time, there were significant changes taking place in CROP's fund-raising activities. Memories differ about where the first CROP Walk took place: some say it was in the Dakotas, others say the East Coast, still others say California. John Metzler Jr., a national staff person in the days when the "Walk" was first introduced, believes that the first walk was organized by Roger Burtner, then Mid-Atlantic regional director, "almost against National

Office" wishes.[6] Burtner gives credit for the walk idea to George Sturgeon, then CROP director for the Dakotas, who suggested to him in 1970 that he try a "novel idea for fund-raising which he had heard about from some Canadian friends."[7] Wherever the first CROP Walk was held, there is no question that the walk has become a major activity of CWS/CROP, and that it has now been used by dozens of other organizations.

It was also Roger Burtner who later organized the first CWS/CROP Work Camp for ten weeks in Africa. Following their time in Ghana, nine of the participants in the Work Camp became "Volunteer Interpreters," sharing with church and community groups across the country their experiences and new understandings about hunger and development. As CROP became more diversified in its fund-raising, it began to provide materials to NCCC member churches for use in vacation church schools. Those materials became widely used in helping children understand more about the issue of world hunger and what could be done about it. Robert Rooker, a former communications director for CROP, remembers that it was also at that time that CWS/CROP began a circulating library of hunger-related films, at that point probably the best and most extensive lending library of such films in existence.

Initially, the films in the collection were mainly on world hunger and were used largely by churches and CROP committees organizing local events. Many of those films were directed and produced by Linda Robbins, then a member of the CROP communications department. Later she became director of CROP communications, and in addition to developing CROP materials, for several years she helped create and produce most of the materials used to promote the One Great Hour of Sharing.

In recent years, as the number of videos in the film library on a wide range of social issues has increased, so has the usage by both schools and colleges, who find the films an excellent resource in their education programs. As CWS and CROP celebrate fifty years, Gary Arnold, film librarian in Elkhart oversees a library that has grown to include some 500 titles, with approximately 5,800 shipments a year. Now with its own e-mail address, the CWS Film Library remains probably the largest free film-lending library on hunger and related social issues available from any private voluntary organization in the United States.

******

The late 1960s were years of social and political unrest in the United States. Nineteen sixty-eight was the year that both Martin Luther King, Jr., and Robert Kennedy were assassinated. It was also the year of the "Poor Peoples March" on Washington, D.C. When hundreds from across the country passed through New York on their way to the nation's capital, Melvin Myers, CWS material resources director, gathered a group of volunteers in the educational building of Riverside Church, where they made 107,000 bag lunches for the walkers to carry with them.

******

For fifty years, one of Church World Service's strongest assets has been the quality of its representatives throughout the world. In the nine years of Vietnam Christian Service, no fewer than eighty-five individuals from CWS served on its staff. Some of them, like Doug Beane and Dean and Margaret Hancock, spent the rest of their working lives involved in relief, refugee, and development activities related to CWS in one way or another. Dennis Metzger continues to work with CWS/CROP as the Illinois regional director. Others like Skip Dangers, Perry Smith, and Bill Herrod are still working in Laos, Vietnam, and Cambodia.

Families, including husband, wife, and children, often went out for CWS. Gary and Carol Ann Ambrose have represented CWS not only in the Ryukyu Islands, but also, from 1967 to 1977, in Korea, Brazil, and Haiti. For more than ten years, they were involved in a variety of activities with an emphasis on community development and responding to "the felt needs of the people," transferring programs "to local control as soon as possible." Then, in 1977, with the rapidly growing refugee resettlement program on the West Coast and the increased interest in the Pacific Basin, the Ambroses finally returned to the United States to open the first West Coast Office of Church World Service. That office was a resource and support to denominations in their relief and refugee work and for the CWS/CROP regional offices already on the West Coast.

Another family that served CWS overseas during those years was that of Ralph and Flossie Royer. Church of the Brethren missionaries in Nigeria, the Royers were asked by CWS to go to Agadez, a provincial center in Niger. Ralph Royer, a specialist in community development, especially in developing water resources, helped start irrigation systems, well digging, and the planting of gardens. Those were new skills for formerly nomadic cattle herders, but they needed the gardens to provide food as they became more settled. One of Ralph Royer's accomplishments was the organizing of work crews that built 100 kilometers of road using only hand tools to clear the land of rocks and bush. Marilynne Hill, retired director of the Christian Church (Disciples of Christ) Week of Compassion, and a longtime member of the CWS Committee, remembers that with Ralph Royer working alongside them, the Tuareg built the road with pick and shovel, eating what was available and sleeping along the side of the road until it was finished. Today, she reports, it is the Tuareg who keep the road up, and have added many branches that lead to various farms.

People like these—the Ambroses and the Royers—and others like them helped make and still make CWS a serving agency of a serving church providing help and hope to untold thousands over the years.

IV

While Church World Service was increasingly undertaking long-term development programs and projects, it continued to respond to major disasters as they occurred. Many of those natural disasters occurred in South and Central America while Dwight Swartzendruber was director of that geographic area office. One of the strongest and most devastating earthquakes of the century struck Peru in May 1970. That quake resulted in the deaths of 60,000 people and destroyed tens of thousands of homes. Entire towns and villages were destroyed, together with much of the infrastructure of the country; roads, bridges, irrigation systems, and communications systems were in ruins.

At the time, CWS was "operational" in Peru: It conducted its own service and material-aid programs, and it did so as a foreign agency rather than working through any local organizations. By being operational, CWS was able to undertake a large-scale emergency response program to the earthquake. It should be remembered that in Latin America in the early 1970s, unlike today, there were few, if any, nongovernmental agencies capable of mounting the kind of relief and development activities that were undertaken in the country, and for that work to be done, being operational was necessary for an agency like CWS.

Jerry Aaker, an alumnus of VNCS and one of the most experienced workers in the development field, was in Peru at the time doing mission work for the Lutheran Church of America (LCA). When the quake struck, he was loaned to CWS and, in the following months, directed part of a disaster relief program that channeled hundreds of tons of relief supplies into the stricken area.[8] Some of those supplies were used in Food-for-Work projects, in rehabilitation and reconstruction activities helping communities in the rebuilding process.

It was not long after the earthquake in Peru, that another major disaster occurred. On December 23, 1972, a severe earthquake destroyed much of Managua, Nicaragua. Church World Service had no ongoing work in Nicaragua but decided to become involved in providing assistance and again asked Jerry Aaker to go there to "mount the relief effort."[9] Before agreeing to that request, one stipulation Aaker laid down was that CWS not become "operational" as it had been in Peru but to work instead through local churches. That decision, readily agreed to by CWS, set the pattern for any future disaster recovery programs in which CWS was to become involved.

The key to the earthquake response in Nicaragua was a medical doctor named Gustavo Parajon. Dr. Parajon was a member of an evangelical church, and by the time a CWS representative arrived he had already called together some pastors of evangelical churches to begin forming a disaster response organization. In Latin America, "evangelical" is the word used to describe most Protestant churches. Out of that pastors' meeting came CEPAD—the Evangelical Committee for Aid to the Victims.

Within a few days after the formation of CEPAD, congregations from the evangelical churches had set up children's feeding stations, and within a week those churches were providing daily food for some 30,000 survivors, and pastoral care to people who had lost members of their families. Under Dwight Swartzendruber, CWS's role was a supportive one, to provide food and other material resources that were necessary during the recovery and rehabilitation stages. Church World Service also made available the services of Jerry Aaker to the fledgling CEPAD. He helped in planning and organizing relief and development operations, and participated in some key decisions that needed to be made. From the beginning, the prime mover and motivator of CEPAD was Gus Parajon, and much of what the organization was able to do in immediate relief and long-term development after the earthquake was due to his vision and Christian commitment.

Four years after the Nicaraguan earthquake, CWS learned of another devastating quake in Central America through the wife of Gus Parajon. From Managua, Joan Parajon asked a ham radio operator to radio to CWS that on February 4, 1976, Guatemala had been hit by the worst earthquake in the history of that region. On the Richter scale it measured 7.6, killing 25,000 people and injuring 70,000 more. Out of a population of six million, one million had been left homeless.

Church World Service's first response was to ask for relief supplies to be sent into the area from Nicaragua and Honduras—both countries where CWS had helped in past disasters. Soon air shipments of food, clothing, medicines, and blankets were on the way, to be followed by shiploads of aid materials. As often happens in such disasters, aid flowed in from many different private and governmental organizations. But, sometimes, once immediate relief needs have been met, many of those organizations leave the area and go on to other things.

However, CWS's experience over the years had shown that people who have suffered through an earthquake, flood, or tornado need help over an extended period as they begin trying to put their lives back together again. Often, the victims of disasters are among the poorest of the area. Their houses are not built to withstand the tremendous forces unleashed by natural disasters, and they usually do not have either the funds or the political power to ensure that what is rebuilt is any stronger or quake-resistant than those that had been destroyed.

That was the situation in Guatemala. Long after the initial aid shipments had tapered off, there were still one million homeless people. There was no question but that the building of secure, livable housing was a priority. Dwight Swartzendruber and Kirk Alliman, CWS associate executive director for emergencies, set about the task of helping the churches of Guatemala in the rebuilding process. The CWS role was to provide funds and some materials to help in that process. The people of the communities were themselves central to the rebuilding process, with each family contributing either cash or labor in the construction of their own homes. Construction was usually cement blocks with zinc-coated steel roofing. Many "stack sack" houses were also built.

Stack sack houses were built by filling sausage shaped sacks with a mixture of sand and cement and putting them in water to harden. They were then stacked one on top of another to make walls, with iron rods connecting them, resulting in a building that was unusually earthquake resistant. Church World Service supplied the materials plus the equipment for efficiently filling the sacks with the required mixture. The people of the community operated the equipment and built the houses.

Church World Service stayed in Guatemala for three years, but the people of the Guatemalan churches played the major role in the rebuilding of their communities. North American churches had provided $4 million toward the reconstruction, and by the end of three years, 20,000 Guatemalans had new homes.[10]

Another part of the world susceptible to natural disasters is Bangladesh. Plagued almost annually by cyclones and tidal waves, Bangladesh remains one of the poorest and least developed countries in the world. After Bangladesh had secured independence in 1971, churches from several countries set up the Bangladesh Ecumenical Relief and Rehabilitation Service (BERRS). An office was opened in Dacca in 1972. With help from Church World Service, the Bangladesh Council of Churches then set up its own agency, the Christian Commission for Development in Bangladesh (CCDB), and by mutual agreement took over the ecumenical program that had begun the year before.

Church World Service had secured a $1 million contract from the United States Agency for International Development (USAID) to build houses in Bangladesh. Because of USAID rules, an American was needed in the country to assure the United States that the AID money was used properly. Howard Jost, a young Mennonite who had been a volunteer when Bangladesh was still East Pakistan, undertook that assignment. During the first year Jost served as CCDB's director, and over the next few years, he worked with the churches of Bangladesh and CCDB in a variety of relief and development operations. Today, almost twenty-five years later, Howard Jost is still part of the CWS staff team working in the New York office.

Besides the AID grant, the churches' activities in Bangladesh involved both relief and development. Some food and clothing were distributed in emergency relief situations. Long-term programs included the replacement of equipment lost during the war for independence or in cyclones, and the building of barges and small ships used to transport grains and other products along the coast and into the many inland waterways. Another program was a rice project using improved varieties secured from the International Rice Research Institute (IRRI) in the Philippines. With the support of the churches, technicians from the IRRI went to Bangladesh to help oversee the project.

Programs that had been begun by the churches and CCDB, including health and other services, provided models for other parts of the country. Eventually many of them became the basis for programs established by the government of Bangladesh.

******

In the mid-1960s, part way through the UN Decade of Development, rapid population growth—especially in poorer countries—surfaced as a major concern for the nations of the world. It was deemed important that developing countries stabilize the growth of their populations. In 1965, the National Council of Churches passed a resolution on the issue of population growth, and in 1973 Church World Service established an office called Family Planning, headed by a former college teacher from the Philippines, Epifana Resposa. The function of the office was to supply information about birth control, and sometimes contraceptives. Tragically, Resposa was killed in an airline crash near Washington, D.C. before the program was well underway. Succeeding her was one of her former students, Iluminado Rodriguez, who with others in the churches, believed the original approach too narrow. On her recommendation, the name of the office was changed to Family Life and Population Planning (FLPP). She was also aware of the fact that the perception of many in the developing countries was that rich countries were telling them to stop having children.

Church World Service had come to the conclusion that the churches needed to show a wider concern for the welfare of a society than just controlling population. That fit well with the primary CWS goal—the improvement of the quality of life for all people. The work of CWS/FLPP demonstrated that belief and showed again how CWS worked with and through local groups. When Lumen Rodriguez encountered a YWCA sewing program in Bangladesh, she suggested that information on health and birth control be included. When the director of that program agreed, CWS provided a cash grant so that the program could be expanded. When the International Planned Parenthood Foundation saw what was being achieved, it assumed sponsorship of the program, and CWS moved on to start a similar program in another YWCA.

V

In 1973, Eugene Stockwell, a United Methodist who had served as a missionary in Latin America, became associate general secretary of the National Council of the Churches of Christ in the U.S.A. and director of the Division of Overseas Ministries (DOM). The debate about the relative merits of relief and development had never been resolved, and shortly after Dr. Stockwell's appointment the governing board of the NCCC directed DOM to develop a clear statement of goals and strategies to make ecumenical organizations like CWS more effective in relating to countries where they had programs and were active.

Church World Service, a part of the DOM, sponsored a consultation in June 1973, at Stony Point Conference Center (New York), on the political aspects of relief and development, under the direction of James MacCracken, executive director of CWS. The consultation, which included DOM and CWS committee members, staff, and representatives from denominations, concluded that CWS had a responsibility to "assist people in their aspirations for self-determination and should seek broadening and more relevant ways of carrying out its ministries so that they will enhance man's opportunity for self-development, liberation and justice." It went on to say that many aspects of CWS service programs were "meaningful illustrations of CWS commitment to systemic change."[11]

Shortly after that consultation, Albert Farmer announced his intention to retire as national director of CROP. After a wide ranging search, MacCracken nominated Ronald E. Stenning to be Farmer's sucessor. He was elected, but that was not to be the end of major staff changes in Church World Service.

What had appeared to be an agreement between the DOM and CWS at the Stony Point Consultation did not last. Soon, the longstanding tension between the "mission" people and the "service" people surfaced again, leading to the resignation of MacCracken in June 1974. In resigning, he stated that his policy had been to get food to hungry people wherever they might be, while others held that the way CWS did that unintentionally gave support to repressive governments.

Nevertheless, in spite of the problems caused by the debate and the resignation of the executive director, 1974 was an important year for Church World Service in many ways. Church World Service had long been aware of the need for representation in Washington on questions of world hunger and on U.S. government policies surrounding that issue. Finding that they had many of the same concerns, CWS and Lutheran World Relief opened a joint Office on Development Policy in the nation's capital. Church World Service agreed to underwrite 60 percent of the cost and Lutheran World Relief, 40 percent. Larry Minear was named director of the office representing the two agencies. He began immediately to provide information on U.S. food policies that enabled the agencies to raise questions about how food was being used by the government. Apparently, often the government was using the threat of withholding food aid to countries that did not support its positions in votes in the United Nations. Both CWS and Lutheran World Relief registered strong opposition to that practice, saying that it punished innocent and hungry people for the actions of their governments.

In the early days of PL 480, Church World Service, Lutheran

World Relief, Catholic Relief Services, and CARE delivered most of the commodities available to voluntary agencies. By 1959, CWS and LWR were allowing their programs to level off, while CRS and CARE programs expanded. Over the years, CWS continued to cut back its use of PL 480 commodities under MacCracken, and by 1974 CWS had reduced its use of U.S. government commodities to 15 percent of the CWS budget. MacCracken had also refused to allow those commodities to be distributed to Vietnamese soldiers by Vietnam Christian Service. While the agency did continue to receive government funds for ocean freight reimbursement and the resettlement of refugees, the use of government commodities was reduced even more—to less than 10 percent in the 1975 budget.

The specter of world hunger had become so widespread that a World Food Conference was held in Rome in November 1974. It was at that conference that the then U.S. Secretary of State made the bold assertion that within the next ten years no child would go to bed hungry, nor would any family worry about where its next meal would come from. Representatives from most nations and Private Voluntary Organizations (PVOs) attended those sessions. Church World Service was represented by Larry Minear, from the Office on Development Policy, and Robert Rooker, communications director of CROP.

An article that appeared in *Worldview* at the time stated that "the way we define the world food problem is critical. The food issue has constantly been put before the American people as a matter of humanitarian charity." But, it went on to say that such a description distorts the problem and dilutes the nature of the moral claim of world hunger. The problem, it said, "was not one of charity but of justice" and raised the question of how the American people decide among competing claims upon their resources.[12] Rooker remembers that it was during that time that CROP materials about world hunger began to take on a different emphasis and began to deal more with root causes of hunger and poverty in the world.

VI

Nineteen seventy-four was an important year for CWS in other ways. Long concerned about the situation in the Middle East and especially Palestinian refugees, over the years Church World Service had established close working relationships with many church leaders in that area of the world. Major conferences on the refugee problem had been held in 1951 and 1956, but events in the mid-1960s added to the problem and increased the willingness of the churches in the Middle East to work together on behalf of refugees. Following more ecumenical meetings, twenty-two Eastern Orthodox, Oriental Orthodox, Anglican, and Protestant churches in fourteen countries formed the Middle East Council of Churches (MECC).[13] While CWS has never sponsored a separate program of its own for Palestinian refugees, it consistently has assisted and supported programs of the MECC, which remains an important colleague of CWS in the Middle East.

Another refugee situation developed when Turkey invaded Cyprus in 1974. The occupation of a large portion of the island left 200,000 Greek Cypriots displaced. In that situation, CWS provided some support for a World Council of Churches and Church of Cyprus refugee service program. Although Greece and Turkey agreed to a cease-fire with Cyprus, emotions continued to run high, and before peace was restored, the U.S. ambassador to Cyprus and his secretary were killed.

******

Closer to the United States, more than 2,500 Haitians had risked the 800-mile trip to Florida since 1972, often in unseaworthy boats to escape the oppressive regime in Haiti. Their arrival again raised the issue of equal treatment for refugees who came to U.S. shores. As far back as the Refugee Relief Act of 1953, the U.S. government had treated people differently depending on their country of origin. Most welcome were those who were escaping communist or communist-dominated countries. Least welcome were those who came from countries with which the United States was allied. The situation in 1974 underscored those differences.

At the time when Haitians were coming to the United States, Vietnamese also were taking to sea in flimsy craft to escape the forces of North Vietnam that were overrunning their country. The United States made a special effort to help the Vietnamese, as it had the Cubans, but it put Haitians in jails and detention centers, refused them work permits, and took steps to deport them. The churches, mainly through the CWS Immigration and Refugee Program, interceded on behalf of the Haitians preventing them from being returned to a country where many of them would face imprisonment and possibly death. Yet, in spite of that, the treatment of Cuban refugees and Haitian refugees who came to the United States continued to be very different.

To provide ongoing support for refugees and their sponsors in areas of greatest concentration, CWS opened refugee offices in San Francisco and Los Angeles and established several offices throughout the country known as Ecumenical Refugee Resettlement and Sponsorship Services (ERRSS). Through those offices, CWS helped fund community projects, provided English as a Second Language (ESL) classes, assisted refugees in securing employment, and helped with job training. By 1976, Church World Service was funding forty-nine ERRSS offices.

******

Although CWS had been responding to disasters throughout the world since its inception, it was not until the early 1970s that the member churches asked CWS to respond to domestic disasters. Originally, five CROP regional directors were trained as disaster response people. When a disaster occurred in the United States, one of them went to find out the extent of the damage and how CWS might best respond. The only restriction was that they could not function on behalf of CWS if the disaster happened in their own region. That system worked quite well for a period. Nevertheless, when a series of tornadoes in the spring of 1974 swept across southern Indiana and virtually destroyed much of the city of Xenia, Ohio, the pattern of CWS response changed forever.

The destruction and the number of deaths resulting from such a massive disaster made it clear that much more needed to be done by the churches than just sending money, clothing, or blankets into a disaster area. It was in Xenia that the first Interfaith Disaster Recovery organization was created. Local churches, with financial help and staff support from Church World Service, formed a new organization that operated not only during the immediate recovery period but for more than two years after the tornado, providing pastoral counseling to bereaved families and in other ways helping people put their lives back together again. When, in 1976, the Big Thompson Canyon flood claimed more than 100 lives and caused millions of dollars in damage, CWS staff and three people from Xenia went to Colorado to help the churches there form their own disaster recovery organization.

VII

A new era in the history of Church World Service began in 1975, with the election of Paul McCleary as executive director. A United Methodist who had been a missionary in Bolivia for many years, McCleary brought a wealth of knowledge and information to the agency that would prove useful in the years ahead. Within a few days of his taking office the army of South Vietnam collapsed, and Saigon was on the verge of falling. At the time, there were more than 120 staff of VNCS still in Vietnam, and the rapid deterioration of the situation broke off any effective communication with them. Through what contact was possible with staff, they were urged to leave the country as best they could. Thousands of South Vietnamese were also fleeing, with more than 130,000 refugees coming to the United States.

Although all foreign personnel had to leave the area, and the official U.S. presence had ended in Vietnam in April 1975, consultations were begun with churches from Western Europe, Canada, Australia, and New Zealand, aimed at a program of reconciliation with the people of Vietnam. The World Council of Churches began a Fund for Reconciliation and Reconstruction in Indochina (FRRI), and CWS provided major support to the fund. In its initial stage, FRRI raised $10 million for work in North and South Vietnam, Laos, and Cambodia. Hostilities had ended, but it would be years before there was to be any effective reconciliation between Vietnam and the United States.

******

Another effort at reconciliation by Church World Service in 1975 was its Ireland program. The conflict over the governance of Northern Ireland had resulted in many dead and wounded, as well as fear and terror for many others. Church World Service became involved because of the religious dimension—conflict and hatred between Protestants and Roman Catholics. Still, another reason was a desire to help Americans with Irish forebears better understand the roots of the conflict and have a means of supporting progress toward a lasting peace. Church World Service's involvement began with a request from the Irish Council of Churches, a request for help in some peace projects it was sponsoring. The request also included an appeal for funds to assist the Irish Council in its work.

In July 1975, the Rev. David Bowman, a Jesuit priest, was employed by CWS as a full-time staff person to work in the project. The first Roman Catholic clergy ever employed by the NCCC on its professional staff, David Bowman established a program to sensitize American churches about what was happening in Ireland, provide resources to support the Irish churches, work of reconciliation, and to take U.S. church leaders to Ireland so that they might gain a deeper understanding of the conflict and the issues involved. During Fr. Bowman's time with CWS, many projects received support and encouraged the people of Ireland to recognize that they were part of a worldwide Christian community that was concerned for them and their welfare.

******

With the coming of Paul McCleary to CWS and Ronald Stenning as national director of CROP, changes began to take place in both organizations. In 1976, the first of what were to become annual meetings of CWS and CROP staffs took place at the Bergamo Center in Dayton, Ohio. Those annual events increased the cooperation between the two units and benefited both staffs. Church World Service staff could provide much needed information about overseas programs and projects for the fund-raising staff, while CROP staff shared information about the interests and concerns of donors and church members in the United States about how their contributions were used by Church World Service.

As 1976 was ending, a paper, "The Fourth Decade," was presented to the National CROP Committee. It proposed a two-year pilot project in what was then called constituency education. Earlier in 1967, the "Manifesto for American Action Against World Poverty," which was reported in *The Christian Century,* had said that the churches could do much more to arouse the American public and to inspire a new constituency on the issues of world hunger and poverty. It called for church leaders to think and act from an international perspective. It was from that perspective that Church World Service materials began to reflect increased attention to root causes of hunger and poverty.

The Fourth Decade proposal called for an experimental program in four CROP regions[14] to decide how best to undertake the important task of increasing CROP's emphasis on education about hunger, poverty, and related issues. The basis for the recommendation was the conviction that as important as financial contributions are for an organization like CWS/CROP, an equally important step in the process of dealing with hunger and poverty is the education—the enlightenment—of people in the so-called developed world.[15]

The kind of educational program envisioned in the proposal

had been carried on for some time by churches and church agencies in Canada and Europe. One objective of the pilot project would be to study those programs and determine if they could be used effectively in the United States. The proposal was eventually approved by the National CROP Committee and the CWS Committee, and in 1977 CROP assumed the additional task of being the global education arm of Church World Service.

******

The International Women's Year, sponsored by the United Nations in 1975, had helped the world to focus on the issue of women's fuller participation in development and in the life of society. Because of its commitments to development and quality of life for all people, the role of women was of particular concern to CWS. Some development programs were having an adverse effect on women. In light of that, Church World Service decided to study and reflect on the impact of its relief and development efforts with an emphasis on the possibility of CWS and related agencies enabling women to participate more fully. To that end, in 1976, CWS sponsored a "Consultation on Women and Development" in India, the conclusions of which were included in a report entitled "But We're Not Afraid to Speak Anymore," edited by Joy Wilkes. That consultation helped shape future development activities and policies of the agency especially with respect to the role of women.

CWS Archives

Vietnamese Boat People in Hong Kong harbor. 1979

CROP Archives

A CROP Hunger Walk in Jefferson City, Missouri. c.1980

R. Stenning/CWS

Children in a Bangladesh refugee camp feeding station funded by the Christian Commission for Development in Bangladesh and CWS. 1975

J. Blankfield/CWS

A disabled child in Sudan learns to walk with the help of a walking frame made through a program supported by CWS.

Mike Pszyk, former director of the CWS/IRP Miami office, greeting arrivals during the Cuban Family Reunification flights of the late 1960s.

Esteban Martin

L. Whalen/CWS

A local artist forming a "Dove of Hope," which became the symbol of resurrection and renewal following the Guatemala earthquake, in 1976.

David Hutson

CWS nurses at Geweha, Ethiopia. 1985

When you reap the harvest of your land, you shall not reap to the very edges of your field, or gather the gleanings of your harvest . . . you shall leave them for the poor and the alien: I am the Lord your God.

Leviticus 19:9-10 NRSV

We should care enough about hungry people to ask why *they are hungry. And if we ask that question, the answer is as simple as it is complex: People are hungry because they are poor.*

Arthur Simon, Founder
Bread for the World

Part Four

1977–1986

As Church World Service approached its thirtieth year, it had long since moved from programs of relief to programs of development. Even in those cases where disasters made relief activities necessary, as in the Guatemala earthquake, attention was focused on the conditions that would exist after the immediate crisis and plans made for the transition from relief to rehabilitation and development.

World events had helped determine the activities and agenda of CWS during its first thirty years and continued to do so as it entered its fourth decade. Emperor Haile Selassie had been deposed in Ethiopia; Cambodia had fallen to the Khmer Rouge forces; military coups had taken place in Bangladesh, Nigeria, and Thailand; while Prime Minister Bhutto had been deposed in Pakistan. Church World Service was to be deeply involved in all of these locales during the years ahead.

Natural disasters were also creating situations of intense human need. Earthquake and floods in the Philippines had killed more than 3,000 and left thousands more homeless. Two earthquakes, less than a year apart, had devastated parts of Turkey. The Jumma

River in India overflowed its banks killing 10,000 people, while a dam burst in Gujarat State swept untold thousands to their deaths. Following the cessation of hostilities in Vietnam, all shipments of food and other aid from the United States ended. Vietnam became plagued by typhoons and floods, and hunger and famine became widespread. These were all situations to which CWS was soon to respond.

I

The opening years in CWS's fourth decade were busy ones. The situation in the Middle East, and particularly the fate of the Palestinians, continued to be a major concern of the U.S. churches. Beginning in 1977, CWS issued appeals totaling $600,000 for aid in Lebanon. Most of that money was received within two years.[1] The funds were used to repair church-related schools and hospitals damaged during the civil strife that had begun tearing at the fabric of the country two years before. Some funds were used to support a village development project that enabled people to remain in their villages rather than moving to Beirut, while others were used to aid a school established by the Middle East Council of Churches to serve children in a predominantly Muslim community.

Nineteen seventy-seven was also the year CWS became involved in a unique way in Turkey. The practice and policy of CWS had always been to work through local churches or church-related agencies. In Turkey, there were virtually no Christians except minority Armenians, Greeks, and Syrians. So, while great pockets of human need existed, there was no church agency through which CWS could address those needs.

With the usual avenues not available, CWS, with several European church agencies, joined a consortium organized by the World Council of Churches to support the work of a new organization, the Development Foundation of Turkey (DFT). The DFT, founded and headed by Altan Unver, a young man born a

Muslim, was established to deal with the problems faced by people in the villages and to help them improve the quality of their lives. The members of the consortium pledged a total of $400,000 a year from 1977 to 1979, with $150,000 of that coming from the United States through CWS.

The program was so successful that it came to the attention of the Turkish government and the World Bank, enabling CWS gradually to reduce its support. Once again, Church World Service had shown the importance of providing initial support to a program while it proved its worth; then CWS stepped aside for the program to be carried on either by a local group or by an international agency such as the World Bank.

Within CWS itself, significant changes were taking place. A Development Office was established in New York to monitor development programs and projects that CWS was supporting worldwide, and to ensure that the programs met the criteria agreed on by staff and the CWS Committee. New CROP offices were opened in southern California and the Pacific Northwest. A Church World Service office was opened in San Francisco to support the activities of denominational offices on the West Coast and to be an information resource for the regional CWS/CROP offices.

CWS and denominational agencies continued to respond to natural disasters. In 1977, a cyclone on the east coast of southern India was followed by a tidal wave that washed away at least sixty fishing villages, killing thousands of people, and causing a great deal of damage inland. Kirk Alliman, who had earlier represented CWS in the Philippines, managed a CWS grant from USAID to build emergency shelters. The provisions of the grant stipulated that those funds had to be used within three months. When they were expended, CWS supported its partner agency, the Church's Auxiliary for Social Action (CASA), in building more permanent housing. Marilynne Hill of the Christian Church (Disciples of Christ), who had spent many years in India, remembers participating in the dedication of the first village to be completely rebuilt with brick houses with the support of Church World Service.

II

Two important activities in the history of CWS began in 1977: the two-year pilot project in constituency education and the Vietnam wheat shipment.

Development education, as it later was called, formally became a part of CROP's mandate in 1974. Besides its longtime function of conducting appeals for commodities and funds, CROP was mandated to "inform and sensitize American people in support of self-development of people around the world." In many ways, that was a fundamental shift in the education efforts of the organization. For many years, CROP staff and materials had been doing an excellent job of sharing information about global hunger and poverty and how contributions to CROP were helping alleviate those problems. In essence, CROP staff had been doing program interpretation.

With the addition of development education to its mandate, CROP moved beyond program interpretation and undertook the more difficult task of helping people discover ways in which domestic and global political and economic policies and practices were significant elements in the perpetuation of hunger and poverty in the world. Part of that learning was the recognition that those living in economically developed countries benefit at the expense of those living in the so-called undeveloped countries. The purpose of the pilot project was to explore how development education could be best accomplished in the United States among church members.

The undertaking of that kind of education by the churches was deemed so important in some countries that a World Council of Churches consultation in 1970 had advocated that 25 percent of all church "development project" funds should be used to underwrite such education activities.[2] While CROP never came close to that level of funding, it did engage a staff person to work with the directors of the four CROP regions included in the pilot project to conduct several experimental programs.

Among the models designed and set up during the two-year project was an Interstate Hunger Conference. It involved some fifty-two church leaders and CROP volunteers from Illinois and Indiana, several in-service training sessions for the entire CROP staff, and an overseas educational experience for seventeen participants from several CROP regions who paid their own way to visit CWS partner agencies and programs in Central America. It also sponsored three consultations of European and American educators in seminaries in Atlanta, Indianapolis, and Claremont, California. One additional model involved sponsoring "One World Weeks" which were patterned on work begun in Canada that tried to involve entire communities, schools, libraries, and churches in development education activities.

A final report of the pilot project led to the establishment of the CWS Office on Global Education (OGE) and the creating of a new unit in CWS—the Community Education and Fund-Raising Unit (CEFR). CROP and OGE became part of the new unit responsible for "all public appeals fund-raising and all education" done on behalf of Church World Service.

To help set the direction and program of the OGE, Ronald Stenning, the director of CEFR, assembled a group of church educators including: Richard D. N. Dickinson, president of the Christian Theological Seminary; Atlee Beechy of the Mennonite Central Committee and first director of VNCS; Ann Beardslee, Hunger Program officer of the Presbyterian Church (USA); and Arthur Simon, president of Bread for the World. This group, with wide experience in both domestic and international church-related programs, became the nucleus of the CWS/OGE committee that would help shape the program in the next few years.

******

In 1977, CROP also played an important role in a major effort undertaken by CWS aimed at Indochina. In response to the famine conditions in Vietnam, CWS decided to send a shipload of wheat to that country. During the war, as many as 1,500 ships a year carried weapons of war and other supplies to Vietnam from the United States. With the cessation of hostilities, all such shipments ended. When the decision was made to send the shipment of food, CROP was asked to secure contributions of wheat in eight Midwestern states and to raise funds for the purchase of additional wheat and shipping costs through its other regional offices.

The wheat was shipped by rail to Houston, and in April 1978, a service of dedication was held. Senator Dick Clark, of Iowa, gave the main address calling the shipment "a symbol far beyond the value of the wheat itself. . . . It said to the world that the American people understand the needs of the hungry who need help." That was the fundamental premise on which Church World Service had been founded three decades earlier.

Several others who participated in the Houston event explained what the wheat shipment meant to them. Harvey Schmidt, a Mennonite farmer from Kansas, said, "I represent the farmers who grew the wheat that we now give to the Vietnamese." Cliff Kirkpatrick, then of the Houston Metropolitan Ministries, saw the shipment as "a gesture of reconciliation between the people of our two nations." Ann Taylor from Elkhart said, "I represent CROP who made the arrangements to collect the wheat and ship it to Houston."[3] In a follow-up to the shipment, eighteen senators, including Hubert Humphrey, who had been so instrumental in the passage of PL 480 years before, sent a letter to President Jimmy Carter calling on him to share surplus grain and rice with the people of Vietnam and Laos.

Although a CBS News poll showed that two-thirds of those polled said they favored sending food aid to Vietnam, the U.S. government did not act. The final cost of the shipment, for which CWS received no ocean freight reimbursement from the United States because the government maintained a trade embargo on Vietnam, was more than $2 million. A delegation of CWS board members and staff, including Harvey Schmidt, the Kansas farmer, and led by Paul McCleary, met the shipment in Ho Chi Minh City (Saigon) in May 1978 and also witnessed its arrival at the final destination where it was milled into flour to be used in hospitals and orphanages.

Following that shipment, the Southern Asia Office of CWS, under the direction of Midge Austin Meinertz, initiated what was to become an annual CWS-sponsored consultation on Indochina that focused the attention of the churches on healing the war's wounds and reestablishing relationships with Vietnam. In that respect, Church World Service was at least fifteen years ahead of the rest of the nation.

III

Refugees continued to be a primary concern of CWS. In 1979, the Vietnamese government agreed that the United Nations High Commissioner for Refugees (UNHCR) could establish an office in Ho Chi Minh City to help people to emigrate to the United States and other parts of the world for family reunification. To help in that process, CWS loaned Michael and Sarah Myers to the United Nations to establish the UNHCR office. They were the first representatives of any U.S. voluntary agency to work in Vietnam since the end of the war in 1975.

That same year, twenty-two camps in Thailand and six in Malaysia provided refuge for Southeast Asians choosing to migrate from Vietnam. Since 1975, the number of refugees who had emigrated either by land or by sea increased from 35,000 in 1976 to more than 200,000 by 1979. The U.S. State Department asked for help from voluntary agencies in documenting refugees, and CWS agreed to establish a Joint Voluntary Agency Resettlement (JVAR) office in Malaysia representing all PVOs serving refugees in the area. By the end of 1979, the JVAR staff included twenty Americans, and some forty to fifty local staff.

Another major refugee population developed following the fall of Phnom Penh, Cambodia, to the Khmer Rouge forces led by Pol Pot. After hard fighting, Vietnamese-led forces recaptured the city, and the horror of the Khmer Rouge was revealed to the world. William (Skip) Dangers, an alumnus of VNCS who is still a CWS representative in Vientiane, Laos, recalls what those days were like. In a recent letter he wrote,

> Those of us on the border saw it all in the faces and the suffering and the deaths that we witnessed. I dare not even try to recall the faces of those children, who traumatized, dehydrated and starved, died right before my eyes. However, I can still vividly picture a small Khmer boy who standing on top of a four-foot high mound of dirt among all that misery was flying a paper kite. . . . The vision of that boy has stayed with me over the years and to me it was a vision of hope and symbolized why we were there.

******

Southeast Asia was not the only region with refugee problems that concerned CWS. In late 1979, a consultation on Palestinian refugees was called by the Middle East Council of Churches in cooperation with the WCC. As a result of that meeting, churches and other groups were urged to "extend and intensify their material aid and other support" of the refugees. In response, the Church World Service committee urged member denominations to increase their support of service programs aimed at helping the Palestinians.

In Africa, meanwhile, the refugee population continued to grow. Within a period of ten years the number of refugees in Africa had increased from one million to four million. In 1979, the United Nations High Commissioner for Refugees (UNHCR) was estimating that the number worldwide had reached fourteen million. Whereas refugee resettlement at the end of World War II had been thought of as a temporary problem, during the lifetime of CWS it had become a major social, economic, and political issue.

By the end of 1980, it was estimated that 3,000 people a day were streaming into Somalia. The eighth poorest nation in the world, it was experiencing a massive influx of people fleeing drought-ridden Ethiopia. Most of the refugees were women and children. Many had died of thirst, starvation, and disease on the way to Somalia, while many who survived the journey were close to death and in great need of medical care. A report that came to the attention of CWS said that in one camp alone twenty children a day were dying of hunger and malnutrition-related diseases.[4]

When the Somali government called upon the international community for help, CWS again worked through a consortium called the Interchurch Response to the Horn of Africa (ICRHA) that included Lutheran World Relief and Catholic Relief Services. The three agencies worked together and built on the strengths of each organization. Each provided $250,000 annually for the three years of the consortium's life. In addition CWS provided water resources and health care, CRS was responsible for food distribution, and LWR worked on the development of agriculture and solar energy. Church World Service also supported the long-range development programs of African churches, such as hospitals, schools, and agricultural development.

IV

The horror of the Pol Pot regime in Kampuchea (Cambodia) was not limited only to the thousands of refugees who fled into Thailand or the deaths of untold thousands of civilians who could not escape. The Khmer Rouge decimated the infrastructure of that country. The economy was in ruins; roads and bridges had been destroyed. There was virtually no communication system, education system, or transportation system left intact. The food deficit was 350,000 tons of milled rice during the four-month period from August to December 1979. Only 10 to 15 percent of the rice paddies in the country were under cultivation; the seedlings needed for planting the next crop had been eaten by people just to stay alive. In the face of that disaster, Church World Service helped form a six-agency coalition, Action for Relief and Rehabilitation in Kampuchea (ARRK).

Mark Schomer, a CWS staff person who served as director of ARRK, wrote in a report in early 1980, "Starvation is definitely unavoidable in the coming months, although assistance from relief agencies will help reduce the number of its victims."[5] In late April, two 45-square-meter barges were sent from Singapore to Phnom Penh to act as floating wharves to receive the 40,000 metric tons of foodstuffs needed per month to prevent the recurrence of famine during the coming summer and fall.

Recognizing the seriousness of the situation in Kampuchea, the White House convened a Cambodia Crisis Committee under the leadership of the First Lady, Rosalyn Carter. The Rev. Theodore Hesburgh, president of the University of Notre Dame, and Paul McCleary, executive director of Church World Service, served as co-chairs of that group. The crisis committee eventually raised more than $90 million for relief in Kampuchea. However, the U.S. government would not allow funds from the United States to be used for development purposes (relief, yes; development, no). So the six-agency coalition that CWS had helped create was limited only to carrying out relief activities.

After the coalition dissolved, CWS continued to work in Kampuchea and arranged funding for development projects to come from churches in Germany. It also arranged through the Cuban Ecumenical Council for teams of hydrologists to restore the irrigation systems and veterinarians to restore health to the water buffaloes and other animals that were so important to Kampuchea's economy.

******

Larry Hollon, then director of Interpretation and Promotion for CWS, remembers his visit to Kampuchea this way:

> Shortly after the Pol Pot regime fell I went to document CWS rehabilitation programs. I saw children so traumatized that they were still in a state of shock. We saw one little boy whose leg had been blown away as he rode a water buffalo to a rice paddy to work. The hospital was little more than an empty

room with old metal beds: no sanitary equipment, no running water, no anesthetics and precious little stores of medicines. CWS had sent medicines and equipment to that hospital.

We went to the killing field where hundreds of people had been murdered. Skeletons were being unearthed as the government continued the gruesome work of getting a census of the dead. Skulls were stacked in triangles and the stench was beyond description. Walking by was a little boy who stopped and talked with us. We learned that CWS had provided paper, pencils and desks for his school so it could begin teaching children again.

In the nightmare of Kampuchea one would least expect to find optimism and hope. But at Ou Dong we found children scouring the fields for spent artillery shells. In backyard forges, artisans melted the casings down and transformed them into small bells. The bells were stitched to the harnesses of oxen and water buffalo and they jingled pleasantly as the animals plowed the fields or pulled wooden carts along the highway.

Larry finished his reflection in this way:

Those bells for me are not only a symbol of the remarkable resilience of the human spirit in the midst of the most oppressive conditions imaginable, but also symbolize the spirit of CWS as a connecting link. Wherever healing and hope is needed most, CWS seems to be present enabling life-changing work to occur. By some miracle it finds those whose spirits soar above the crushing conditions of war, disease and destruction and helps them to help themselves and their communities to overcome. It finds people who can turn artillery shells into bells. In the tiny tinkling sound of those bells, I am reminded of the power and strength of the ideas behind this global community, and somehow I am always reassured.[6]

What better tribute to an agency of the American churches that for fifty years has brought help and hope into the lives of millions.

V

Nineteen seventy-nine was an important year in other ways. It was in that year that a working document entitled "The Nature of Church World Service" was released. That staff paper explained in considerable detail several important aspects of Church World Service:

- the theological rationale for its existence;
- to which agencies, churches and persons it related;
- the fundamental goals toward which its work was directed;
- guidelines for CWS activities;
- its areas of special consideration.

That document made clear that the common goal of all that CWS does is based on the belief that human well-being depends on the interplay of the spiritual, social, and material aspects of life. While it recognized that life is not possible without basic physical necessities such as adequate food or shelter, it held that the quality of human existence cannot be measured exclusively in terms of material goods. The work of CWS is grounded in the conviction that a life of quality for all people results when fundamental moral and ethical values are present in the social, political, and economic dimensions of public and private life.

Since its founding in 1946, CWS has been providing the basic physical necessities of life: food, clothing, blankets, and medicines to meet human needs in an ever-increasing number of situations around the world. Its activities over the years had fallen within the scope of its original mandate: (1) immediate relief in response to human need caused by disasters of one kind or another; (2) meeting the needs of refugees and displaced persons either within their own country or providing resettlement to those who were forced to leave their homeland; and, (3) development: working to overcome situations of underdevelopment caused by various factors.

For the first time, in the "Nature of Church World Service" working paper, CWS stated two additional functions it saw as integral to its ability to fulfill its primary role of enhancing the quality of life: constituency (now global) education and public policy advocacy. The education emphasis was seen as enabling CWS to increase its U.S. constituency's understanding of the root causes of hunger, poverty, and other symptoms of human need, while public policy advocacy would allow CWS to share with public officials the insights it had gained through its worldwide relationships and activities.

Since the Office on Global Education was created, education has become institutionalized in the life of CWS. Materials produced by the OGE have been used not only by churches but also in schools, colleges, and seminaries. Through OGE, Church World Service has become known as a leader in the field of development education. The influence of OGE has been felt in many ways beyond the church community: for example, as founder of the annual World Food Day, and as a consultant to the Biden-Pell Educational Grant Program. Also, OGE materials such as its Fact Sheets have been distributed to all members of Congress concerning pending legislation on issues like child-prostitution and anti-personnel landmines.

The Office on Development Policy (ODP), since it was established by CWS and Lutheran World Relief in 1974, has spoken often on issues in which the two agencies have special expertise. Over the years it has exercised leadership in both the religious and Private Voluntary Organization (PVO) communities. One of its contributions has been to stress ethical and moral arguments rather than self-interest arguments in foreign aid debates. An annual series of staff enrichment meetings was held in Washington to inform the staff of the office's activities and some of the issues it was addressing. The keynoter at the first of those meetings was Senator John Danforth of Missouri, an Episcopal priest, who had just returned from a fact-finding trip to Africa. His description of the conditions he had seen in refugee camps and elsewhere contributed to an increased emphasis on Africa by CWS.

A constant goal of the ODP has been to seek increased funding for humanitarian aid. Larry Minear, director of the office, was a founder of the Interreligious Task Force on U.S. Food Policy which later became Interfaith Action for Economic Justice. As the work of the ODP became widely known in Washington, staff members Minear and Carol Capps were often asked by congressional staff to participate in the formulation of legislation dealing with development assistance issues. Through the Office on Development Policy, CWS and LWR were the first private agencies to share with administration officials and members of Congress their experiences in overseas relief and development programs, information that in some measure helped influence national policies and legislation on those matters.

One indication of the role ODP staff exercised in Washington was Minear's invitation to serve on a White House staff team to help develop options for President Carter's initiative on overcoming world hunger. Minear would later serve as a staff member on the Presidential Commission on World Hunger. Another staff person, Cheryl Morden, provided leadership and participated with representatives from other PVOs in a coalition that developed a document proposing new directions for U.S. economic policy toward Central America.

Both the Office on Global Education and the Office on Development Policy continue to play important roles not only in the agency itself but also in church-related and PVO national forums on education and public policy issues.

Nineteen seventy-nine was also the year in which Iranian students seized the U.S. Embassy in Iran. Sixty hostages were held for over a year and not released until the end of the Carter presidency. Church World Service staff played a significant role during that time. Richard Butler, CWS Middle East director, who had first gone to that region in 1960, arranged for the hostages to have a Christmas Day visit by three U.S. clergy: William Sloane Coffin, senior pastor at Riverside Church (New York City); William Howard, president of the National Council of Churches; and, Bishop Thomas Gumbelton of the Roman Catholic group, Pax Christi. Butler accompanied the three clergy to Teheran and visited with the hostages. Both he and Charles Kimball, a future CWS Middle East director, had contact with the Iranian students during the time they occupied the U.S. Embassy.[7]

VI

The changing conditions in Eastern Europe led to reopening contact with the churches in Poland. Church World Service had been involved in a program with those churches for many years following World War II, but had earlier ended its assistance programs when it appeared that aid was no longer needed. By the late 1970s, deteriorating conditions in Poland caused CWS to have conversations with the Polish Ecumenical Council. During a visit in early 1980, it was determined that the time had come to reopen the assistance program, especially to provide sterile hypodermic needles, and much-needed repair parts for U.S.-manufactured medical equipment such as dialysis machines. Several communities in the United States, with many people whose families had emigrated from Poland, conducted special appeals for CWS to purchase and ship (by air freight) repair parts, medical supplies, shoes, and other needed items to Poland.

Meanwhile, a new Cuban refugee crisis was developing. In 1980, more than 100,000 Cubans landed in Florida as part of the Mariel boatlift. Most of those who came were ordinary people who wanted to make new lives for themselves in the United States, but there were some who had criminal records and histories of mental illness. The influx of such large numbers, and the kind of problems some of them obviously had, presented major problems to the state of Florida and for a resettlement agency. In response to that emergency, Mike Pszyk, the longtime director of the CWS Immigration and Refugee Office in Miami, trained more than 100 new staff persons to be assigned to refugee camps in Fort Chaffee, Arkansas; Indiantown Gap, Pennsylvania; Camp McCoy, Wisconsin, and the two Krome Detention Centers in Miami, Florida. It was from those locations that sponsors were found for most of the Cubans.

During that same year, more than 7,200 Haitians also sought refuge in the United States. The U.S. government maintained that the Haitians were economic rather than political refugees. That was another example of the different way in which refugees were treated in this country. By May 1980, only sixty of the estimated ten thousand Haitians had been granted political asylum.[8] Church World Service continued to object to the classification of Haitians as economic refugees and brought suit against the government on their behalf. When a federal judge ruled in favor of CWS and the NCCC, CWS began to seek sponsors for Haitians in this country.

Church World Service, with other members of the American Council of Volunteer Agencies (ACVA), also objected to the decision of the Carter Administration to move Cuban and Haitian refugees to Fort Allen, Puerto Rico, claiming that the move was a violation of the international Protocol on Refugees. A challenge to the administration's plan resulted in the Supreme Court ruling that the government was within its rights to use Fort Allen as a refugee processing center. At that point, CWS and other agency representatives met with government officials and informed them that if the move to Puerto Rico took place, they, as refugee resettlement agencies, would not cooperate in any way. That was not the last time that the government decided refugees from Cuba and Haiti should be processed offshore from the United States.

The 1980 Refugee Act, the product of a two-year study of U.S. immigration laws and policies by a "Select Committee on Immigration and Refugee Policy" resulted in two major objectives long advocated by CWS. First, it established a comprehensive policy for refugee admissions into the United States; and, second, it created a domestic policy of resettlement assistance that was the same for all groups of refugees. Church World Service officials had testified before the Select Committee and in congressional hearings during the formulation of the 1980 Refugee Act.

From its earliest days, when Roland Elliot had testified for the 1948 Displaced Persons Act, through the 1960s and 1970s when John Schauer and Nancy Nicalo had administered CWS/IRP, Church World Service had seen its work with refugees as a cornerstone of its overall program. Efforts by CWS and other PVOs had, over the years, helped shape the country's immigration and refugee policies. Those efforts were probably more effective than similar efforts to influence and shape U.S. foreign aid policies. Between 1946 and 1980, more than two million refugees had been admitted to the United States, and during those years CWS had, with the help of the member denominations, resettled more than 350,000 of them. Even in 1980, faced with the unequal treatment of Haitians, CWS helped resettle more than 13,000 refugees in all fifty states. Of those, 18,467 were Indochinese, 8,192 were Cuban, 564 were Haitian, and the remainder were from Europe, the Middle East, and Africa.

It was in 1979 that CWS began what were to become annual meetings with representatives of the German churches. In some thirty years, Church World Service had come full circle. Some of its first activities were to provide relief supplies for the people of Germany and to help in the rebuilding of their churches. Now the meetings of representatives of American churches with those of German churches brought together two groups committed to global emergency relief and long-term grassroots development. It was through those meetings that funds from the churches of Germany were made available for development programs in Kampuchea undertaken by CWS in the early 1980s.

VII

Member denominations had experienced some decline in membership during the 1970s and consequently were less able to contribute to ecumenical and nondenominational programs. The fund-raising efforts of CROP became increasingly important in the support of Church World Service activities. The 1974 World Food Conference alerted many people to the seriousness of global hunger, and people both inside and outside the churches wanted to help. Fund-raising methods were changing. Even within rural areas, canvassing farm-to-farm, house-to-house was becoming less effective.

One of the most widely used educational and fund-raising tools of CROP to dramatize the disparity of wealth and resources among the people of the world was the Third World Meal. Participants were divided into several groups. One group received a typical American meal, a second the kind of meal found in less developed countries, and a third group received the meager amount of food available to people in what the United Nations had designated as the Least Developed Countries (LDC) of the world. Those dinners, often held in cooperation with Church Women United, received much more media coverage than a rural canvass ever received. People became informed. Consciences were awakened. Attitudes were changed. As one participant said, the dinners not only dramatized the great disparity between resources available to people but also moved them to want to share with those who were living on the edge of daily survival.

Another idea had proved fruitful: the CROP Walk. The idea had taken hold on the East Coast and soon spread to other parts of the country. The Mid-Atlantic Region had held its first walk in 1971, and by the next year there were fifty-five CROP Walks up and down the Susquehanna River Valley. The Ohio region hired two Future Farmers of America to organize walks in that state, and Michigan also began to use walks as an educational and fund-raising tool. By the mid-1970s, besides walks, other sponsored events were being used. Lowell Brown, the Illinois regional director, rode his bike the entire length of the state while sponsored bikers joined him as he rode through their areas.

In June 1975, CROP had been selected as the organization to represent in the nation's capital what was being done by PVOs to combat hunger and malnutrition through relief and development programs around the world. Roger Burtner and Wes Albin organized a bike trek from Washington, Pennsylvania to Washington, D.C. The riders arrived in the capital on a Friday evening. After meeting with congressional leaders the next day, the riders and their bikes joined in the procession at a service—held at the National Cathedral—that focused on world hunger. Ronald Stenning preached the sermon.

In 1979, which had been designated by the United Nations as "The Year of the Child," CROP produced a series of audiovisuals designed especially for young people to be used in churches and vacation church schools. They were intended not only to help youngsters in the United States understand the reality of world hunger and poverty, but also to make the joy of giving come alive. Those widely used tapes and filmstrips helped children relate experiences in their own lives to those of children in refugee camps and in less-developed parts of the world.

The CWS Clothing Program that had been administered by CROP since 1960, especially the Blanket Program, had become an increasingly important source of income. Offering envelopes were made available and "Blanket Sundays" were held in churches across the United States. For a donation of $4 (later $5), CWS could buy a wool blanket directly from the manufacturer. Whenever a disaster struck, in the United States or elsewhere, first shipments included blankets: each year more than 300,000 were sent into disaster areas. Often they were a person's only protection from the weather; it was a carry-all in which a homeless family could gather up a few salvaged possessions; and often a CWS blanket provided some privacy within a crowded refugee camp.

Many women's groups participated in the CWS Clothing Program by assembling Sewing Kits of precut children's clothing and layettes, and by providing hospital supplies such as rolled bandages and hospital gowns. Young people's groups also assembled school kits and health kits to be used in clinics and schools throughout the world. Once told of the needs, such groups responded magnificently, and there were few programs that gave such a direct link to the lives and well-being of women and children in other parts of the world. It has been estimated that 70 percent of the world's refugees are women and children, and the gifts of clothing and layettes were among the most welcome items CWS ever sent.

During those years regional CROP offices continued to be established. On the East Coast, once covered by Ralph Taylor alone, offices were opened in upstate New York, New Jersey, New England, the Mid-Atlantic, Virginia, and the Carolinas. Pennsylvania was divided into east and west, and the Office on Global Education was moved from Elkhart to Baltimore. Because the activities of CROP and Bread for the World (BFTW) were mutually supportive, and so many participants in CROP events were members of BFTW, discussions were held about opening a joint office in Denver to serve the Rocky Mountain states. Because of legal and other concerns, that office was not opened but both organizations continued to be mutually supportive. Arthur Simon, president of BFTW, served on the CWS/OGE committee and CWS staff were on the BFTW board of directors.

To support the nationwide network of CROP offices, the Elkhart office facilities were expanded with the addition of a new warehouse to house materials, films, and other items needed by regional offices. With Hattie Redmond responsible for inventories, and David Hoke and Cyndy Comment-Woods in the warehouse, thousands of boxes of supplies are sent from Elkhart each year to CROP offices and CROP-event organizing committees throughout the country.

With the increase in the number of CROP offices and the amount of public-appeal funds CROP was raising, concerns were expressed by some in national church bodies about whether funds received in CROP events should be given to local churches and then sent to the denominations. To address that and other issues, representatives of constituent denominations and CROP officials met at a two-day consultation. Participants concluded that CROP was becoming an increasingly important source of income for Church World Service, and that its appeals were aimed at the larger community and not primarily at church members. Clearly, those who sponsored participants in CROP events were usually family members and neighbors who would not have given the money to a local church. It was also agreed that denominations should inform their local judicatories that "CWS and CROP were an expression of ecumenical cooperation," and that they should urge their members to participate in local CROP events.

In the early 1980s, Church World Service joined with Catholic Relief Services and the American Jewish Joint Distribution Committee (AJJDC) to form the Interfaith Hunger Appeal (IHA). Lutheran World Relief soon also joined in. It was envisioned as an ecumenical, faith-based fund-raising effort. However, CWS, through the efforts of the OGE staff, urged that any fund-raising be accompanied by education. Within a short period, the goal of IHA was expanded to include not only raising funds to combat hunger and poverty overseas but also to do so through education and awareness raising in the United States. One activity of IHA was the Thanksgiving Hunger Fund Appeal, believed to be the first joint educational and fund-raising effort ever undertaken on the national level by major Protestant, Roman Catholic, and Jewish organizations aimed at the general public.

In response to "Directions from Nairobi," a report from a 1979 CWS-sponsored consultation, CWS had committed itself to a special three-year emphasis on Africa from 1980 through 1983. And, in 1983, as the situation in the Horn of Africa continued to deteriorate, CWS issued a special Global Hunger Appeal for $6 million. CROP offices undertook the challenge of raising a substantial portion of that appeal. As the American public became increasingly aware of the tragedy unfolding in Ethiopia, the goal of the appeal was met and then extended to $10 million. Eventually, the appeal topped out at more than $17 million, fully supported by churches and individuals between the years 1983 and 1985.

In 1985, the famine in the Horn of Africa became the focus of a major international relief effort after a filmclip from the British Broadcasting System was shown on U.S. television. To CWS, with its long history in Africa, and its earlier involvement in the Interchurch Response to the Horn of Africa (ICRHA), the 1985 famine came as no surprise. Educational materials and special appeals were designed to inform church members of the disaster and the overwhelming needs in Africa and to raise funds to meet some of those needs.

CWS's country offices were gradually phased out as national churches began supporting some forms of Christian service. One means of maintaining contact with those newly emerging churches, while withdrawing from immediate involvement in service programs, was to create a regional structure. Because it was one of the world's neediest areas, Africa was the first area selected for a regional office. An office was established in Nairobi for East Africa and the Indian Ocean. From that vantage point, CWS could provide enormous amounts of needed food, medicines, clothing, seeds, and tools to people in the drought and famine stricken parts of Ethiopia. When transportation of supplies within the country became a problem, CWS used some funds raised for the Ethiopian crisis to provide trucks so that aid could reach people in remote areas.

******

Besides aid supplies, CWS also recruited medical teams to work in the refugee camps in Somalia. Roma Jo Thompson, a former CROP regional director, volunteered to work in the Ali Matan camp as a trainer of Somali women and to cook and care for the doctors and nurses in the medical teams. She remembers the medical staff as "a caring, giving group of people some of whom went from crisis to crisis serving" in similar situations of human need. One fond memory she has of her time in Ali Matan was seeing crates of food and blankets marked "From CWS" come into the camp. Today she recalls that it was like some of "home" had been sent to help them in their work. It was not just those working overseas who were part of that response to the tragedy taking place half a world away. Brenda Rendall of the Elkhart office remembers the abundance of mail that arrived during the Ethiopian crisis. She wrote recently, "I still can't believe how generous people from all over the country were during that time. The love that was shown during that crisis is what Church World Service is all about."

VIII

During the late 1970s, CROP-raised funds were being used by CWS to support specific program activities overseas. A list of "Program Categories" had been agreed to and annual amounts assigned to each category: food, seeds and food production, water resource development, building materials and equipment, and appropriate technology. This latter category was particularly important, as technology and equipment that were used in the United States and other developed countries was often inappropriate in less developed areas of the world. CWS and partner agency staff knew thousands of pieces of farm equipment and pumps sent overseas by well-meaning groups lay idle because there were no spare parts to keep the equipment running. Gas-powered pumps to provide water were useless without fuel to run them. Materials needed to build elaborate food-storage warehouses were not available in the very places they were needed. So CWS staff, with local church and partner agencies, determined what kind of technology was appropriate for a particular task and CROP funds were used to make it available.

CROP funds were also used for People to People Opportunities (PPOs). Specific programs overseas were identified as needing support, and CROP regions were asked to raise and provide funds for those projects. Among the dozens of such PPOs was a Methodist Health Clinic in Chile that assisted children at high risk for prostitution and helped to rehabilitate those who had been prostitutes; a program called "Popular Education in Health" sponsored by the Evangelical Church in Chile; a "peasant shelter" for rural people fleeing violence from paramilitary groups in Colombia; and, a program for women providing vocational training in sewing, baking, and local crafts. Like the layettes and kits of the clothing program, those PPOs were a direct link between people in CROP regions and people overseas.

During the late 1970s CWS decided to allow up to 25 percent of all funds raised in a CROP event to be returned to the community in which they were raised. As hunger and poverty increased in the United States in the early 1980s, that policy took on new meaning. CROP-raised funds began to be used on a truly global basis. CROP organizing committees decided which food pantry or hunger-fighting agencies in their community should receive funds and, following the event, up to 25 percent of all that was raised was sent from Elkhart to help support those local programs. Since 1948, participants in CROP events had had the opportunity to designate their contributions to accredited overseas agencies other than CWS. With the additional policy of having 25 percent returned to a local community, CROP was making its events not only ecumenical but also was meeting the needs of those concerned with both domestic and overseas hunger and poverty.

In spite of its best efforts to meet human need throughout the world, CWS had its critics. The television program *60 Minutes* and the magazine *Readers Digest* used the time of the crisis in the Horn of Africa to mount a double-barreled attack on both CWS and the National Council of Churches under the title, "Do You Know Where Your Money is Going?" By selective reporting and interviews with longstanding opponents of ecumenical agencies and foreign aid, they portrayed CWS and the NCCC as radical groups supporting all kinds of subversive and questionable activities in Africa and Latin America. The public response, especially from more conservative groups within and outside the church, was deafening. Editorials appeared calling for clarification and answers to the charges that had been made.

In many ways those attacks were a blessing in disguise. As questions poured into New York and Elkhart, they provided an opportunity to talk about CWS and CROP, about what had been done over the years, and how the money that had been contributed had actually been spent. CROP staff across the country had opportunities to speak before church and other groups, such as Kiwanis and Rotary meetings, that had not been available to them in the past. Thanks to the attacks, there was more public interest in what was being done by CWS and what the NCCC stood for than there had been for years.

As Church World Service approached the end of its fourth decade, there was another change in leadership. In 1984, Paul McCleary, who had led the agency through some of its most crucial years, resigned to accept a position in his own denomination, the United Methodist Church. Richard Butler, who had been filling the dual roles of Middle East director and CWS operations officer, was selected to become executive director.

Meanwhile, significant program initiatives were underway in both Africa and Latin America. In Senegal, the Keur Momar Sarr projects became some of CWS's most successful development initiatives. Through those projects people were provided with skills and received training that enabled them to bring about lasting changes in their own lives. Upon his return from Senegal, Butler recounted talking to a Muslim farmer in Keur Momar Sarr who welcomed him as if he were a member of his family. "When any member of the family comes home," the farmer said, "we all rejoice." It was apparent, Butler said, that a deep bond of understanding existed between me, representing CWS, and this farmer. Both recognized the oneness of the human family and felt deeply those bonds of common love and responsibility that hold us together.

In Latin America, the São Paulo Process had begun, representing a model for a new and different north/south relationship. It began when representatives of sixty-four programs and projects in Latin America and the Caribbean met with members of the NCCC/CWS Latin America office for mutual evaluation. Although Church World Service and the churches had long been active in that area of the world, the goal of the São Paulo Process was to change practices and relationships that had been in place for many years. An ongoing exchange between the New York office and its regional counterparts enabled decisions to be made jointly. The full impact of the São Paulo Process was to be felt in the years immediately ahead.

It was in the mid-1980s that Church World Service became a separate division of the National Council of the Churches of Christ in the U.S.A., and the executive director of CWS became an associate general secretary of the Council.

******

The highlight of the 1986 staff conference was the appearance of John Metzler Sr., a founder and first national director of CROP. Speaking of those early years, he recalled "shirtsleeved men laboring to stack piles of food around the altars of their churches, women who had sewed garments for relief and assembled supplies for hospitals bringing them to church as their offering, and communities piling up a mountain of wheat for relief in the town square." It was in those days that the Church of the Brethren purchased an entire college campus in New Windsor, Maryland, and transformed it into a service center for the processing of relief supplies. Metzler recalled seeing a truck loaded with tons of ready-to-ship folded clothing and bedding leave New Windsor every night for the port of New York.

With the increased amount of mail and packages, the New Windsor post office had to be upgraded and the railroad had such a problem with schedules because of the heavy shipments that they began putting materials destined for processing in New Windsor in express cars that were simply uncoupled there to await unloading.

Those were "heady times," Metzler recalled. The Episcopal Church designated a million dollars from the Presiding Bishop's Fund specifically for handling material aid. Metzler told of a conversation between the Arthur Morgans of the Tennessee Valley

Association and the Danforths of Ralston Purina. Mrs. Morgan said to Mrs. Danforth, "Your company makes food for dogs and cats, can't you devise a good food for hungry children and adults?" The result was a specially formulated cereal. That product, with reconstituted powdered milk, was widely distributed for institutional use in Italy, Greece, France, Germany, and Poland. It was never placed on the retail market in the United States.

In closing, said Metzler, "We can't go back. It's up to you in today's world with today's problems and today's resources to find ways to direct Church World Service toward what it ought to be now."

******

The ecumenical nature of CWS was evident not only in the diversity of its staff but also in those who chaired the CWS Unit and Department Committees through the years. Besides Harper Sibley, a businessman from Rochester, New York, who served as the first chair, in later years the leadership came from individuals from a variety of positions and denominations. These included David Taylor of the Presbyterian Church, Muriel Webb and Marion Bingley of the Episcopal Church, J. Harry Haines of the United Methodist Church, William Thompson, Presbyterian Church (U.S.A.), Bishop Philip Cousin of the African Methodist Episcopal Church, Alfred Bartholomew, United Church of Christ, and Robert Marshall, Lutheran Church in America.

Several programs that began in Church World Service were transferred in the mid-1980s to other church-related organizations. The Christian Medical Commission, originally established by CWS, later became part of the World Council of Churches. Mel Myers, director of the Material Resources Program (MRP) of CWS, started a similar MRP office for the WCC in Geneva, and CWS gradually turned over much of its worldwide activities in providing material aid to the WCC and the Commission on Inter-church Aid, Refugees, and World Service (CICARWS). Similarly, a number of local organizations became the core of ecumenical bodies in countries where Christians were a minority. Church's Auxiliary for Social Action (CASA) in India and Christian Commission for Development in Bangladesh (CCDB) in Bangladesh are two examples of how CWS, in partnership with local churches, assisted in helping indigenous organizations get started. Church World Service then supported those local ecumenical agencies until they could become independent. Partnership has always been, and continues to be, a hallmark of Church World Service and one of its most important defining characteristics.

L. Robbins/CWS

Fresh water flows from a gravity-fed irrigation system in Madagascar, built by local villagers with help of FIKRIFAMA, a CWS colleague agency. 1985

L. Hollon/CWS

Inoculating livestock in Cambodia after local Khmer were trained by Cuban veterinarians with funding from CWS. 1980

R. Stenning/CWS

Young man in a vocational training program operated by CEPAD in Nicaragua, with support from CWS. 1981

R. Stenning/CWS

Tornado damage in Xenia, Ohio, where CWS helped establish the first Interfaith Disaster Response Organization. 1974

G. Arnold/CWS

All ages take part in a CWS/CROP Walk in Elkhart, Indiana, location of the national CWS/CROP office. 1980

. . . they shall all sit under their own vines and under their own fig trees, and no one shall make them afraid . . .

Micah 4:4 NRSV

CWS has several characteristics I have always valued . . . there was always a strong emphasis on mutual respect and mutual responsibility in responding to the challenges of poverty and hunger.

Kathryn Wolford, Director
Lutheran World Relief

Part Five
1987–1996

The opening years of the fifth decade in the life of Church World Service continued to be turbulent ones. Governments and their leaders were under siege in many places. Anti-government riots took place in Haiti, and "Baby Doc" Duvalier fled to France. Ferdinand Marcos left the Philippines, and the worst riots in decades took place in Karachi, Pakistan. United States and Libyan armed forces clashed. American hostages were held in Lebanon, and one was eventually killed. In South Africa many died in riots in Soweto. There were anti-government demonstrations in Chile, and President Ronald Reagan ordered emergency aid for the Honduran army. People in the United States watched the Iran-Contra scandal unfold.

Through all of the upheaval, CWS continued to work at its goal of helping people everywhere to achieve a greater degree of self-reliance and dignity. One of the most important awareness-raising initiatives CWS undertook during the mid-1980s, was the production of a series of films and TV public service announcements (PSAs) that showed people in need as dignified human beings rather than the kind of pitiful, helpless children and adults too often portrayed in many fund-raising spots shown on television, in promotional magazines, or in direct-mail appeals.

Produced by Larry Hollon, those films expressed the belief that all are the children of God; they afforded their subjects dignity and respect. The films soon had a significant impact on the way other Private Voluntary Organizations (PVOs) began to portray their work. An article by Hollon, "Selling Human Misery," denounced what he called the "pornography of relief." The article originally appeared in *The Christian Century* and received wide circulation in the PVO community.[1]

By the beginning of the fifth decade of its life, Church World Service, including both domestic and international personnel, accounted for more than 80 percent of the National Council of Churches in both staff and budget.

I

At the annual staff conference in the summer of 1987 in Kansas City, CWS sponsored a Fortieth Anniversary Symposium with the theme, "Sharing the Struggles of the Poor: A Challenge to the U.S. Churches." That gathering of CWS staff from around the world, denominational representatives, guests (U.S. and international), and resource people from a variety of disciplines discussed what a future-oriented ministry for Church World Service would look like. Fifteen working groups were asked to identify issues that CWS should wrestle with and to suggest appropriate actions for the organization to take. The symposium was intended to chart the future of CWS for the next ten years. Out of those deliberations came forty-three recommendations either for action or key issues the participants felt needed to be addressed. Central to many recommendations, endorsed overwhelmingly by colleague agency representatives from around the world, was the belief that as important as it was for CWS to continue its work in relief and development activities in other countries, equally important was an expansion of its efforts at the education of the American people.[2]

Global education had moved from being an experiment to becoming a fundamental expression of the CWS program in the United States. Much the same could be said about the Office on Development Policy in Washington. Throughout the symposium, the participants raised the issue of an expanded role for CWS in both education and public policy advocacy. Shortly before the symposium, Larry Minear had written an essay, "Reflections on Development Policy: A View from the Private Voluntary Sector," for a book exploring the role of PVOs in development. That essay, with materials from the Office for Global Education and geographic area offices, provided ample grist for the participants as they wrestled with questions about the future direction of Church World Service.

Following the symposium, CWS established a Global Hunger and Development Fund to "provide resources for community-initiated and community-based programs in food production and distribution, primary health care, social and economic development, and education and advocacy programs concerning the causes of hunger." Monies from that fund helped underwrite activities of the geographic area offices including effective long-range development programs in countries such as Somalia and Senegal.

******

A CROP Walk, organized by Joe Trower, the Missouri regional director, was part of the fortieth anniversary celebration in 1984. Elenor Vieth, a former secretary in that regional office, was recognized during the event for walking ten miles at $100+ per mile on her seventieth birthday. A decade later, in recognition of CWS/CROP's upcoming fiftieth anniversary, she walked in a CROP Walk on her eightieth birthday and raised $15,785. She has promised, "God willing," to do it again on her ninetieth birthday.

II

It had long been the policy and practice of CWS not to become "operational" in its overseas programs. Instead, its goal was to provide funding and technical support when necessary to local churches and church-related agencies as they planned and initiated programs that people in those communities had agreed upon. Recently Kathryn Wolford, first Church World Service regional representative for the Caribbean, and now executive director of Lutheran World Relief, wrote,

> CWS has several characteristics I have always valued: "With the emphasis on supporting indigenous organizations . . . there was never any question of becoming operational . . . always there was a strong emphasis on mutual respect and mutual responsibility in responding to the challenges of poverty and hunger.

By the mid-80s, following the closing of many individual country offices in favor of regional offices that related to large areas of the world, the development work of CWS was largely carried out through the round-table process. Annually, representatives from national councils of churches and partner agencies within a geographic region of the world would gather to discuss mutual concerns and recommend which programs and projects within the region should be supported by Church World Service. A representative from CWS would attend the round-table discussions and take the regional recommendations back to New York. These recommendations would then become part of the overall funding process.

In 1986, the consultation in São Paulo, Brazil, began a process that significantly changed the relationship between CWS and its colleagues throughout Latin America and Caribbean. The consultation brought together representatives from both the New York office and the Latin America and Caribbean churches. Both groups sought to increase understanding of one another's "realities" and "worldviews" in hopes of enhancing true partnership. Earlier, two meetings had been sponsored by the WCC Commission on

Inter-church Aid, Refugees and World Service (CICARWS). One was held in Larnaca, Cyprus, in 1986, and the other in El Escorial, Spain, in 1987. Those meetings focused first, on the necessity for local participation in any development process, and second, on the sharing of ecumenical resources. Oscar Bolioli, director of the Latin America and Caribbean office, said the São Paulo Process was an effort to put these emphases into practice.

Jane Sullivan-Davis, CWS representative in the Andean Regional Office in Santiago, Chile, wrote recently that the São Paulo Process changed the way a CWS regional office works. The openness, the dialogue, and the mutual affirmation allow a regional office to truly "accompany" the partners in the region, while being available for advice and support when needed.

At the time this new process of strengthening relationships with ecumenical partners, particularly in Latin America, was getting underway, political turmoil and human need escalated in Central America. Through its partner agencies in Honduras, Nicaragua, and El Salvador, CWS provided funds for food, shelter, clothing, and relocation assistance to thousands of families displaced by violence throughout the 1980s.

******

Increasing violence, hunger, and hardships of all kinds were also realities in many places in Africa. In Mozambique, 100,000 people had been killed by South African-backed forces since 1985. Drought revisited Ethiopia, threatening to destroy the first signs of recovery from the devastating drought and famine of 1984–85. Church World Service resumed emergency assistance, while maintaining its commitment to long-term development efforts in that country. Work in Ethiopia was a prime example of the philosophy of CWS that while development activities were central to its mission, relief work could not be ignored or neglected. In the Sudan, where as many as two million people had been displaced by civil strife, and where an estimated one million people had died since 1983, CWS made available 1,400 metric tons of food to the Sudan

Christian Council (SCC) for distribution in areas cut off from food supplies.

During 1988, CWS helped move the largest quantity of relief food delivered to southern Sudan. Staff of the Sudan Christian Council (SCC), with assistance from CWS, managed to get convoys of food trucks from Kenya through Uganda, and into Juba and other areas of southern Sudan. The mission was fraught with perils: roads were mined and hostile armies were scattered throughout the area.[3]

Meanwhile, CWS's Malagasy partner FIKRIFAMA, was providing technical assistance to the people of a village in the rice-growing hills of central Madagascar. To obtain clean drinking water, the staff of FIKRIFAMA, with the support of CWS, helped them plan and build a badly needed water system. Community volunteers laid pipe from a spring in the hills to a reservoir and from there into taps in the village.

Recently, Gaston Razafinanja, a native of Madagascar and now CWS/CROP regional director in Wisconsin, visited four rural villages where, twenty-five years earlier, he had installed the water systems. In recalling that visit he wrote,

> The water systems are still working! Trained young villagers maintain them. The fountains are fenced for protection with colorful flowers surrounding them. Villagers report that the accessible water allows children to attend school instead of spending their days fetching the family water. Water-borne disease no longer endangers life.[4]

The kind of technical assistance CWS helped provide in Madagascar (and other places) was also central to its work in Kampuchea, the only place in southern Asia where CWS was operational in the late 1980s. Because the Khmer Rouge had destroyed the country's infrastructure, CWS had no option but to establish its own operations in Kampuchea. CWS programs focused on increasing food production. At a vegetable seed production station, seed stock was improved and local Khmer were trained to run tests and compile data on the results. Vaccinators were trained by Cuban veterinarians, while Cuban hydrologists helped restore water systems and canals. All of this work stemmed from CWS's long-term commitment to rehabilitate Kampuchea.

Natural disasters continued to demand attention from CWS. When 28 million people were affected by the worst floods in Bangladesh's history, CWS immediately airlifted relief supplies to its partner agency, the Christian Commission for Development in Bangladesh (CCDB). In 1988, CWS also responded for the first time to a disaster in the Soviet Union. When Armenia was devastated by an earthquake, which killed 50,000 people and left 500,000 homeless, six shipments of medical and other supplies were sent to the Armenian Apostolic Church and the Evangelical Baptist Churches. Ann Beardslee, a member of the CWS delegation to Armenia, remembers:

> It was a new experience for the Soviets to be open to outsiders like CWS giving material aid to disaster survivors. Yet it was a familiar, basic rite for Christians from one nation to unite with Christians of another.[5]

Closer to home, Hurricane Gilbert, followed closely by Hurricane Joan, swept across the Caribbean, Mexico, and Central America. Nicaragua was hardest hit; there, Joan caused $800 million in damage. Church World Service provided clothing, blankets, and medical supplies, valued at more than $270,000, to Nicaragua and more than $550,000 in cash and material aid to the Caribbean Conference of Churches to help that partner agency respond to emergency needs in the Caribbean.

Simultaneously, a long drought had affected farmers in a large section of the southern United States. Many of them were small landowners who did not qualify for help from existing government programs. Working through state and local councils of churches, CWS established a "farmer-to-farmer" program in which farmers in northern states not affected by the drought shipped hay, seeds, and other supplies to those in the South who were in danger of losing their animals and occasionally their farms through crop failures and foreclosures.

******

In a year of increased need in the United States and many disasters in other parts of the world, more than 3.1 million people in the United States participated in or contributed to CROP events. During its first full year of operation, the Florida CWS/CROP Office helped organize events in twenty-three communities. Janet Young of the Greater Chicago Office, organized a global education conference attended by more than 200 people. A record 1,832 community events were held, most of them walks; sixteen of those walks raised more than $50,000 each. In 1988, income from CEFR public appeals and CROP Walks accounted for more than 50 percent of all income to Church World Service.

For the CWS Immigration and Refugee Program, 1988 was a year of mixed blessings. On the upside, CWS helped find new homes for more than 7,000 people; many new arrivals were Pentecostals from the Soviet Union, where *glasnost* had been extended to cover immigration policies. On the downside, employer sanctions in the 1986 Immigration Reform and Control Act took effect, resulting in increased unemployment in several parts of the country. Without jobs, many people from Central America and elsewhere faced hardship and hunger. More than $118,000 of CWS emergency funds were allocated to ecumenical agencies around the country to meet the needs of undocumented immigrants.

Also, in 1988, the Office on Global Education produced its first book. Entitled *Make a World of Difference: Creative Activities for Global Learning*, it was intended for denominational and community audiences and explored issues related to world hunger from a global perspective. The book sold out its first run of 5,000 copies in the first four months of 1989 and had to be reprinted.

While 1988 was, in many ways, a good year for CWS, it was another year of leadership change. The serious organizational and financial matters that had faced the staff and unit committee for the past three years had not been resolved. During this time of internal difficulties, Dick Butler, the executive director, and Larry Hollon, director of Interpretation and Promotion, resigned. Staff changes and budget restrictions also resulted in the closing of several offices in New York, including the Development Office and the Family Life and Population Program.[6]

III

In June 1988, Ann Beardslee, who had been serving as an associate director of CWS, became executive director. Prior to joining CWS staff, Beardslee had been on the staff of the Presbyterian Church (U.S.A.) and a member of the Church World Service Unit Committee. She assumed her new responsibilities at a critical time.

For several years, two disaster office staffs had worked for CWS and its member denominations—one international and the other domestic. In 1989, financial considerations made it necessary to merge the two disaster response offices under one director.

Involvement in emergency relief activities following disasters had been part of the CWS mandate from its inception. Both the original Certificate of Incorporation and the original bylaws of CWS stressed that fact. In the early 1970s, CWS had been asked by member denominations to act for them in responding to domestic disasters as it had done for years overseas. As its competence in responding domestically was recognized, CWS reached an agreement with the American Red Cross and the Federal Emergency Management Agency (FEMA) about its role in domestic disasters.

As part of its overall domestic response program, CWS trained a cadre of Disaster Response Consultants (DRCs) located throughout the United States. They are individual church members trained to provide assistance to churches and ecumenical agencies in responding to crises in the wake of natural disasters or those resulting from human actions. In 1989, CWS responded to forty-three disaster situations—thirteen of them in the United States—in which the Disaster Response Consultants played significant roles.

With its long history of responding to human need in the wake of disaster, it was important that CWS retain that capability, both internationally and domestically, on behalf of the American churches. When a disaster occurred somewhere in the world, WCC/CICARWS in Geneva would issue a Disaster Appeal to its global ecumenical partners. As a matter of tradition and practice, CWS would agree to underwrite a significant portion of that appeal and then share the appeal with its member denominations. The denominations would respond by sending their contributions to CICARWS through Church World Service.

Faced with an increasingly difficult financial situation, the NCCC Executive Committee levied a surcharge on all CWS expenditures, including those monies denominations and other U.S. agencies "passed through" CWS in response to global disaster appeals and support for overseas development projects of partner agencies. As a result, several denominations and major U.S. church agencies began sending their funds directly to Geneva or to overseas development projects. This adversely affected CWS's programmatic capabilities.

While the CWS Unit Committee understood the Council's need for funds, it was important for CWS to maintain its integrity and not allow any monies entrusted to it to be used for purposes other than those for which they were intended by the donors. Two special meetings of the Unit Committee were held in Chicago to discuss the relationship of CWS to the NCCC and to decide its future status within the Council. After much discussion, it was decided that as a church agency it was important for CWS to continue as a part of the National Council of the Churches of Christ in the U.S.A. if its integrity in financial and other important matters could be assured. During this time, some larger denominations began to develop bilateral relationships in their support of overseas programs, largely bypassing CWS and lessening their financial support of ecumenical activities. The Episcopal Church Presiding Bishop's Fund for World Relief and the United Methodist Committee on Relief are now registered as separate Private Voluntary Organizations (PVOs) with the U.S. government.

However, the relief and development work of CWS could not wait for internal administrative and organizational matters to be resolved. While committees and task forces continued to discuss the future of CWS and its relationship with the National Council of Churches, the important work of meeting human need went on.

In Africa, the need for food in several countries remained acute. In Sudan, Ethiopia, Mozambique, Angola, and Liberia—all facing the devastating trauma of civil war—human suffering was intense. Working through its partner agencies, CWS supported programs aimed at food relief and vocational training for young famine victims. All of those programs were designed to introduce youngsters to better prospects for the future in spite of their present circumstances.

Elsewhere, Southern Asia had then the largest concentration of refugees in the world. Church World Service supplied tents, food, soap, tea, and blankets through the Inter-Aid Committee in Pakistan, where more than three million refugees from Afghanistan were still awaiting repatriation. Church World Service, at the same time, attempted to respond to needs of people in the Middle East. Its principal partner, the Middle East Council of Churches (MECC), distributed CWS medical supplies and blankets to those affected by the massive artillery barrages in Lebanon in early 1989.

Also that year, the Latin America and Caribbean Office initiated a major campaign to aid "children in danger." It had been estimated by UNICEF that 50 million children lived on the streets of Latin America.[7] The campaign was aimed at addressing and communicating the needs of those street children. A CWS-sponsored consultation in Brazil, on the plight of homeless children, drew church and community leaders from throughout the region. As part of its effort to focus attention on the needs of street children, the Latin America and Caribbean Office commissioned Larry Hollon, now an independent filmmaker, to produce a film entitled, *Hope is The Last Thing to Die.* That film, which received wide distribution, told the story of those millions of youngsters living in packing crates or under culverts whose lives are a matter of daily survival.

IV

In many ways, 1990 was an important year. Ann Beardslee, who had served as executive director since mid-1988, retired. She was replaced by Lani Havens, who for four and one-half years had worked with the National Council of Churches in Kenya (NCCK). Among her responsibilities in Kenya was coordinating convoys of food into Ethiopia and Sudan. While in Africa, she had become familiar with CWS through the East Africa Office in Nairobi. In assuming her new position, Havens completed what she called, "the circle of partnership" in the global family.[8]

However, new leadership was not all that CWS experienced that year. The committees and task forces that had been working on the future of CWS and the reorganization of the NCCC recommended the creation of a new entity, bringing together Church World Service, the International Affairs Commission, and what remained of the Division of Overseas Ministries, into a new unit to be known as "Church World Service and Witness" (CWSW). As part of the merger, it was agreed that because of the well-established identity of "Church World Service" and the significant ability of that name to raise public funds, the name "Church World Service" was to continue. A further understanding was reached that as a nonprofit corporation under the laws of the State of New York, "Church World Service, Inc.," would remain the legal organization for the acquisition and disposition of public and governmental funds. Ann Beardslee, in her final report as executive director to the CWS Unit Committee, had underscored the importance of maintaining the name and the legal status of CWS and CWS, Inc. in any new entity that might be created.[9]

An important lesson learned from the discussions about the relationship of Church World Service with the NCCC, and earlier with the DOM, was the necessity of preserving CWS as a Private Voluntary Organization (PVO), together with all the prerogatives that are part of that legal status. It was particularly important that that status be maintained to enable the CWS/CROP U.S. regional network to meet both federal and state regulations in its fund-raising activities. Through the years, organizations raising funds from the general public have come under increasing scrutiny by government regulators and every effort has been made by CWS to meet standards that often vary from state to state. With the creation of Church World Service and Witness (CWSW) it was important that the NCCC and CWS come to an understanding and agreement about these matters.

For the world at large, and particularly for the Middle East, 1990 was a critical year. On August 2, Iraq invaded Kuwait. That invasion—and the resulting flights of Asians, Palestinians, and Egyptians from Iraq and the Persian Gulf States—resulted in a humanitarian crisis of immense proportions. It also caused an exodus of foreign workers from Kuwait and Saudi Arabia. Many of these workers attempted to make their way to Jordan, by way of the vast desert of western Iraq and eastern Jordan. Hundreds of thousands found themselves stranded and in need of assistance. Among the first to respond to that crisis was the Middle East Council of Churches (MECC), which issued an international appeal to its partners, including CWS.

Besides responding to the MECC humanitarian appeal, CWS also urged the United States and other governments to work for a peaceful solution to the crisis. CWS's Middle East colleagues argued that a war in the region would have a terrible human impact: heavy loss of life and a major refugee crisis. When the United States determined to deploy additional troops in the area as part of Operation Desert Shield, the NCCC governing board passed a CWS-sponsored resolution condemning the invasion of Kuwait, but at the same time arguing for a regional solution to a regional issue.[10] An op-ed piece in the New York Times stated that the U.S. churches had "claimed the high moral ground."

During and after the Gulf War itself, CWS turned to the humanitarian challenges created by the war. To escape the wrath of Saddam Hussein, approximately 1.5 million Kurds from northern Iraq had sought refuge in Turkey and Iran. Church World Service provided assistance in both places. Unlike other agencies, CWS refrained from using U.S. government transport and assistance. Looking back on that period, Dale Bishop, then CWS Middle East director, wrote,

> I am struck by the way the crisis brought out the strengths of CWS's mode of working through partner agencies. Our response not only brought assistance to people in distress, aid that was administered by local people, it also strengthened our partner churches in the region.[11]

Because of its decision not to accept assistance from the U.S. government, and because of the need for additional funds, CWS issued a special appeal to support its work among refugees and others affected by the Gulf War. Using an olive branch as a symbol of peace, and a symbol of God's continuing faithfulness even in face of catastrophes, an "Olive Branch" appeal was initiated. That appeal exceeded its goal of $1 million and made possible the provision of shelter, food, bedding, water, medicines, and other supplies to those displaced by the war.

Rapid political change had opened up many new opportunities for service through the churches of Europe. Due to the collapse of old economic and political systems, many of the most vulnerable who lived in Eastern Europe were in dire need of help. Church World Service had already provided $1.25 million in aid to the Armenian people following the 1988-90 earthquake and ethnic conflict. Mobile health clinics, medicine, blankets, clothing, and powdered milk were all part of the material aid sent to help in that recovery effort. At the same time, food, medical assistance, and clothing were provided for distribution by the churches in Romania following the revolution there.

******

Faced with many demands for help from around the world, the Overseas Personnel Office, under Paul Yount, had undertaken a major recruitment and deployment challenge. By the end of 1989, CWS had twenty-four staff members working with local church partner agencies around the world. Some of those staff members served as CWS representatives in regional offices, others as part of emergency response teams in places like Sudan, and still others as medical consultants or as members of a medical team. One of the challenges in 1990 was to recruit and field emergency medical teams in Liberia after that country's civil war. Doctors and nurses with experience in Liberia came forward from the United Methodist and Lutheran churches, supported by volunteers from the Mennonite Board of Missions. By the time the CWS emergency medical teams in Liberia were able to turn over the work to local staff, fifteen doctors and nurses recruited by CWS Overseas Personnel had served in that country.

V

As the 1990s unfolded, CWS continued its important public policy work. In Washington, the Office on Development Policy became one of two North American nongovernmental organization (NGO) members of a Working Group on the World Bank. The NGO group hoped to find ways for more collaboration between NGOs and the World Bank and engage the World Bank staff in dialogue about some of its policies. The Working Group was a strong critic of some of the bank's policies and pressed the bank hard to make information more accessible and to be more participatory in some of its programs and activities. The ODP focused on several key issues, including the reconstruction needs of countries emerging from conflict in Africa and Central America; a "demilitarized" U.S. foreign-aid program for the post-Cold War era; government policies affecting the environment; and foreign aid proposals designed to increase people's participation in economic and development strategies.

Meanwhile, the Office on Global Education published its second major book, *Tales of the Heart: Effective Approaches to Global Education*. Using materials and experiences from workshops conducted by OGE staff both in the United States and in other countries, the book, coauthored by Loretta Whalen and Tom Hampson, was a resource for schools, church groups, community educators, and others who wished to design community-based global education seminars. Another resource for schools and churches produced by OGE in 1991 was a curriculum on hunger and children's rights entitled, *Children Hungering for Justice*. By the early 1990s the OGE was a key part of CWS and the Development/Global Education activities of InterAction. Its staff also led workshops on global education at the World Council of Churches Assembly in Canberra, Australia.

In 1991, a record 334,580 people participated in 1,856 CROP Hunger Walks across the country. Because of the policy of returning up to 25 percent of funds raised in a community to help finance local hunger-fighting efforts, that year more than 3,700 local food banks received checks totaling $3,172,255 from CROP Walks. Sam Ryburn raised $6,772 in the Greater Charlotte, North Carolina Walk. That brought his seven-year total to $36,000. Bobby Hodge, legally blind and confined to a wheelchair, crossed the finish line in Farmville, North Carolina, with pledges from as far away as Finland.

Leah Marsh, a resident of Lonaconing, Maryland, had led member churches of the George's Creek Ministerial Association and local residents in CROP Hunger Walks for twenty-two years. Now, in time for the CWS Fiftieth Anniversary, she is leading them again in her twenty-third walk. The walks were not limited to the United States. On a visit to China, Gene Wei, Presbyterian pastor from San Jose, California, got four members of Beijing's Haidian Christian Church to go on a CROP Walk with him.

Other CEFR public appeals set records in 1991. The CWS Blanket Program topped its old record with $2.96 million and a new effort, "Partners in Tomorrow's Promise," in its first year received pledges of $562,741 from 109 new partners. CEFR, through CROP events and other public appeals, provided more than 59 percent of all Church World Service income in 1991. The longtime practice of collecting good, used clothing through the CWS Clothing Appeal had ended in 1990, and contributors were asked to refocus their energies on more self-help kits and layettes. Experience had shown that the kits and the layettes were needed most.

Key staff changes continued to occur. John Schultz, who had become CEFR director in 1985, resigned, and Doug Beane, a longtime CWS staffer and alumnus of VNCS, became acting director for the next three years.

VI

Church World Service first became involved in Yugoslavia in 1957, when together with Lutheran World Relief it participated in a feeding program in 14,000 public schools for 1.8 million students under the age of thirteen. Later studies showed that the food supplied by the two agencies had made a significant difference in the health of the children. In the early 1990s, CWS again became involved in that part of Europe by providing humanitarian aid for victims of warfare that had broken out in the former Yugoslavia. One of its first acts was to give $1 million through UNICEF during the "Week of Tranquility" in November 1992 for blankets for children caught in the conflict. In addition to a total of $1,441,000 for blankets, medicines valued at $1,330,000 were supplied through clinics ministering to refugees and the wounded. A September 1992 report on the situation in the former Yugoslavia suggested that CWS, working with the WCC, was the major PVO refugee agency "that is significantly and consciously serving the needs of all refugees displaced by the civil war in the Balkans: Muslims, Croatian Catholics, and Serbian Orthodox."[12]

Newt Thurber, then European Office director, writes of the excellent cooperation CWS received from Interchurch Medical Assistance (IMA) and from the Community Education and Fund-Raising Program (CEFR) in putting together the needed supplies. Because CWS had no colleague agency in the area, it was necessary for CWS to open its own office in Metkovic, Croatia, from which to distribute food to displaced persons in central Bosnia and Herzegovina. As had long been the policy and practice, even in that demanding situation the staff in the office were largely local Croatian young people with a minimum number of staff from the United States. By working with USAID and other government agencies, CWS had made it possible by 1993 to provide more than $15 million in aid to those in need in the former Yugoslavia. Of that amount, more than $8 million was contributed by the churches through CWS. During that year, CWS/IRP also resettled nearly 400 refugees from Bosnia in the United States.

Nevertheless, CWS was active in more than just supplying relief aid and resettling refugees. It helped make possible an interfaith conference in Hungary to promote reconciliation and a just peace settlement in the area. CWS staff also met with United Nations and U.S. State Department officials about sanctions in the former Yugoslavia, an issue of major concern to the churches in the region.

******

The southern United States became a focus of attention during the early 1990s because of natural disasters and the rapid influx of refugees into Florida. When Hurricane Andrew—the most powerful storm to ever reach the mainland of the United States—hit Florida, a CWS Disaster Response Consultant was on the site within twenty-four hours. Not only was this a natural disaster in the usual sense, but it was complicated by the fact that there were some 700 Haitian refugees in Homestead and Florida City, two of the hardest hit areas. The combined efforts of the CWS Disaster Response Office and the CWS/IRP Office were aimed at locating the refugees as well as addressing the unmet needs of all the storm victims.

Within a few hours supplies from CWS began to arrive: 1,250 family-size tents, 6,000 cotton blankets, 6,000 health kits, 6,000 flashlights, 1,000 school kits, and 672 portable toilets. Yet in the midst of providing the usual list of material aid supplies, one special need surfaced. A young child in the area with a breathing problem was dependent on respiratory equipment that needed electrical power to operate. Without the respirator the child would be in serious trouble and could die. The CWS Material Resources Program (MRP) under Soon Young Hahn located an electric generator and shipped it to Florida in time to save the child's life. Again, as it had shown many years before in the case of Tanya, the life of one child can be as important to CWS as any of the major programs it supports worldwide.

The Haitian refugees in Homestead were part of the group that had fled their homeland before and following the September 1991 military coup that ousted President Aristide. Thousands had set sail in flimsy craft of all kinds for the United States, where the debate renewed about whether the Haitians were in fact refugees who, according to the UNHCR definition, had a "well-founded fear" of persecution, or economic refugees whose migration from Haiti resulted from poverty, unemployment, and a declining economy. Eleven thousand Haitians were eventually screened into the United States, and Church World Service entered into a contract with the U.S. government to provide initial resettlement services for 4,700 of them. When Andrew struck, 500 had been resettled out of Florida and 700 in the Homestead area.

During that same period, Cuban "rafters" began arriving in increasing numbers. In September and October 1992, more than 1,000 Cubans had arrived in Florida, the largest influx since the

Mariel boatlift of 1980. Those new arrivals were immediately transported to Miami from the Keys where most had landed, and many of them were assigned by the U.S. Justice Department to CWS/IRP for processing and possible resettlement. The presence of large numbers of Haitians and Cubans again focused much of the IRP effort in Miami. Because of the long process required to be granted asylum in the United States, providing legal services to the large number of Haitians, in particular, again put a severe strain on the limited financial and staff resources of CWS.

Over the past decade, the CWS Immigration and Refugee Program has been a leading voice in urging humane treatment for those seeking a safe haven in the United States. It has continued to advocate for an end to the backlash against immigrants in the United States and for amendments to anti-refugee legislation before Congress. Church World Service IRP has attorneys on staff both in New York and Miami to help provide much-needed legal aid to refugees seeking asylum. As the number of refugees coming to the United States continued to rise, and the need for legal assistance and advocacy increased, CWS/IRP reopened its IRP Washington Office. The focus of that office has been on refugee-related issues such as asylum, welfare, health care, and U.S. refugee policies.

The practice of the United States had become one of interdicting Haitian refugees at sea and forcibly repatriating them to Haiti, in spite of their claims of fear of persecution. The United States then began to use the Guantanamo Naval Base and Panama as "safe haven" sites for both Haitians and Cubans. By mid-1994, about 22,000 Haitians were at Guantanamo, and Church World Service, together with other church groups, raised strong concerns about the living conditions at the camps. It was also during that year that the United States changed its Cuban refugee policy. Approximately 30,000 Cubans were picked up at sea and taken to Guantanamo. Unlike past years, resettlement of Cubans in the United States was no longer assured. With thousands of Haitians and Cubans in what was in reality a detention camp, the longstanding U.S. commitment to refugee protection was eroding.

After a series of U.S. policy changes, which included allowing Cubans and Haitians with severe medical problems to be evacuated to hospitals in the United States, all the Haitians except a few unaccompanied minors and those who were HIV-positive and their families, were returned to Haiti. In another change of policy, the United States allowed the majority of Cubans in Guantanamo to be paroled into the United States. With that change, Church World Service and the U.S. Catholic Conference began providing resettlement opportunities for those Cubans, most of whom rejoined families in south Florida. Working with those refugees, CWS/IRP and its ERRSS affiliates provided in-depth community orientation, job-skills evaluation, employment, and job training both in Florida and in other parts of the country where Cubans were resettled.

While the CWS/IRP Washington Office was focusing on refugee-related issues, the Office on Development Policy staff was chairing two coalitions pushing for a U.S. foreign-aid program in which poverty alleviation, environmental protection, and human rights were top priorities. Director Larry Minear resigned to become part of the Humanitarianism and War Project at Brown University. Carol Capps, longtime associate in the ODP, became director of that office. In meetings with the Secretary of State and in congressional hearings, Capps, with other ODP staff members, urged policies that would alleviate poverty and hunger. On behalf of CWS and LWR, ODP was advocating the redirection of United States aid to Central America toward reconciliation, reconstruction, and democratic participation. Cheryl Morden of the ODP staff provided leadership in the coalition that developed a document proposing these new directions.

After a long search, Mel Luetchens, director of Interchurch Ministries of Nebraska—who remembers having gone as a child with his parents to a CROP ingathering in the late 1940s—was selected as the director of CEFR.

When her three-year term as executive director was completed, Lani Havens left the agency and was replaced by Lawrence (Lonnie) Turnipseed, a former missionary and director of the Southern Asia Office.

VII

Willis Logan, director of the Africa Office, wrote that 1993 "was a year of promise and challenge in Africa."[13] He cited the promise of greater democratization in South Africa on the one hand, and the challenges presented by the continuing civil strife and natural disasters in Angola, Liberia, Somalia, and the Sudan on the other. In Somalia, as needs changed from basic relief to rehabilitation, CWS reestablished a base of operations in Mogadishu in cooperation with local partners and initiated several projects that included health care and water resource development. Still, peace did not come easily to Somalia, and the intervention of U.S. troops in a peace-keeping effort was a bitter experience for many Americans. Church World Service also supplied urgently needed food, blankets, and other relief supplies valued at more that $800,000 to Sudanese refugees residing at Kakuma camp, in Kenya, and in Uganda.

All across Africa, CWS and its partners struggled with the ongoing tension between promoting sustainable development and at the same time responding to civil emergencies and disasters. At few times was that struggle more evident than in responding to the 1994 crisis in Rwanda. The Rwandan tragedy left several hundred thousand dead, produced more than three million refugees, and displaced hundreds of thousands of people within their own country. As part of a coalition of agencies, and in cooperation with the Christian Council of Tanzania and the Church of Christ in Zaire, CWS responded to the needs of Rwandan refugees in Tanzania and Zaire, and within Rwanda itself.

******

Two accounts about Somalia and Rwanda must be told.

After a visit to Somalia, Larry Hollon wrote in an issue of his publication *Storyline,* "If all you know of Somalia is terror, famine and poverty, I want you to meet competent, caring Somalis doing humanitarian work at great risk to their own lives."[14]

He described some of those he had met:

> Those who pass through minefields to vaccinate children; those who travel to distribute seeds and tools on roads where bandits ambush and kill; who cross an old battlefield littered with live artillery shells to reach peasant farmers; who stayed to inoculate cattle upon which poor families depend for survival, even though hostile militiamen told them to leave or be shot.

"To many," he wrote in a recent letter, "Somalia is now cited as a failure of diplomacy and humanitarian response. Church World Service is proving it isn't."

The situation in Rwanda was brought into focus by several actions. Willis Logan worked in cooperation with the WCC in 1994 on the Rwandan crisis, CWS issued an appeal, and Lonnie Turnipseed was one of ten people sent on a Presidential Mission in 1994 to gather information and advise the President and the National Security Council on the situation. Three CWS/CROP staff—Doug Anderson, David Bower, and Joe Trower—visited Rwanda in 1995. In their report they wrote,

> We visited the Ntarama church where 5,000 died violently as they sought sanctuary. We listened intently as survivors told their stories. Then on to the CWS-assisted Nyamata high school where children, orphans of the tragedy, began a choral concert sung in the local language. Suddenly, in honor perhaps of visiting U.S. Christians, a hymn rang out in English. The beloved text so caught us off guard that immediate tears flowed—a song so poignant amid such numbing grief and loss, it will never be heard again in the same way.[15]

******

In Southern Asia, East Asia and the Pacific, CWS continued to be involved in various development projects. In those regions, CWS gave priority to helping councils of churches in their development efforts, supporting vital work.

One of the most effective long-term programs supported by CWS for many years has been in Indonesia. In that widespread archipelago of 17,000 islands, where more than 85 percent of the population is Muslim, Church World Service, under the faithful oversight of Nancy Robinson, worked with the Participation in Development program of the Communion of Churches. This program brought Christians together to improve the quality of life in the broader community. Projects in Indonesia included primary health care and nutritional training, water resources, food production, credit awareness and small loans.

Church World Service also supports the National Council of Churches in Korea, the National Council of Churches in the Philippines, and the Pacific Conference of Churches. In China-related activities, CWS provides teachers of English for the Amity Foundation, the agency through which CWS works in China, while also sending funds for disaster relief and to support the development efforts of ecumenical partners in that country.

In Latin America and the Caribbean, the São Paulo Process, begun in 1986, has shown solid results. Peru and Colombia joined efforts to confront violence and human rights abuses, while programs in Chile and Ecuador were organized to begin receiving refugees. Church World Service has supported Agro-Aquaculture and Fisheries projects in Bolivia, Colombia, Ecuador, Honduras, Haiti, and Peru. In 1993 those projects produced 22.5 tons of fish from freshwater ponds and lagoons, providing communities with high-protein food and employment. Those projects are a living example of the old adage that teaching a person to fish is more important than feeding a person for a day.

Because of its support for the restoration of democracy in Haiti and its work with Haitian refugees, Church World Service was one of the few agencies invited to accompany President Aristide on his return. Gordon Summers, president of the NCCC, was also among those in the party that joined Aristide. In response to emergency needs following three years of political turmoil, CWS organized a network of partners to help with recovery efforts in Haiti. These efforts addressed health, education, agricultural development, and other needs.

Church World Service has a long history of working with the churches of Cuba and the Cuban Ecumenical Council. Earlier, this relationship had resulted in Cuban technicians and veterinarians working in Cambodia. Church World Service IRP had also been instrumental over the years in arranging family reunification flights so that persons could be flown from Cuba to rejoin their families who had come to the United States years before. In 1995, under a special humanitarian license from the U.S. government, CWS completed its thirty-fifth air shipment of medicine and other supplies to Cuba bringing the total value of goods shipped to $683,818. Church World Service has always responded to actual needs, including emergency requests for specific medicines not available in Cuba for individual patients. One such request this past year was for a cancer medicine for a two-year-old child. The medicine was hand-carried into the country by Oscar Bolioli to assure its safe delivery.

VIII

As Church World Service approached its fiftieth year of bringing help and hope to people around the world, the challenges it faces have not abated. Wars (or continuing civil strife) in many places—Rwanda, Chechnya, the former Yugoslavia, to name but a few—caused great human suffering. Hundreds of thousands of refugees and displaced persons were driven from their homes by the fighting. Twenty-three disasters required the attention of the Emergency Response Office (ERO) in 1995. The

ERO sent more than $4 million in cash and almost $7.3 million in material aid for worldwide disaster relief and recovery. International emergencies included an earthquake in Japan; floods in China, Korea, and India; and hurricanes in the Caribbean. In the United States, ERO disaster consultants worked with churches and ecumenical agencies in responses to the bombing of the Federal Building in Oklahoma City, flooding in California and southwest Florida, and Hurricane Opal on the U.S. Virgin Islands. In response to the Oklahoma City tragedy alone, CWS provided more than $400,000 to the interfaith response effort.

The challenges CWS faced in 1995 included the proposed actions of a newly elected Congress—a Congress that announced its intentions to severely limit the number of refugees allowed into the United States—to bring about sharp reductions in foreign aid, and further reduce U.S. commitments to multilateral action. Congress also tried to place new restrictions on nongovernmental organizations in their advocacy efforts with the government.

Faced with those possibilities, the Office on Development Policy in Washington mounted extensive efforts to protect funding for programs under attack. In partnership with other faith-based and secular nongovernmental organizations, CWS was instrumental in preventing wholesale cuts in development aid, including programs that combat world hunger.

Of particular concern to CWS was proposed legislation affecting refugees and immigrants in the United States—legislation that would separate families, divide communities, and endanger children. Among the provisions of the proposed legislation was the slashing of U.S. commitment to refugee protection by imposing a cap of 50,000 on annual refugee admissions and enacting new restrictions on asylum and humanitarian parole. Following a ten-month effort, in which Elizabeth Ferris, director of the CWS Immigration and Refugee Program, provided important leadership, the Congress voted to delete the annual 50,000 person-gap, as well as other cuts in legal immigration. Working with Episcopal Migrant Ministries and Lutheran Immigration and Refugee

Services, CWS/IRP helped organize a nationwide network of concerned religious groups in a "Campaign for Refugee Protection." Following the action of the House of Representatives, Elizabeth Ferris said, "After months of incredibly hard work by thousands of church advocates across the country, it's a true blessing to see these tremendous results."

In the face of increasing anti-immigration feeling in some parts of the United States, one of the biggest challenges facing CWS/IRP was responding to the needs of Cuban refugees. The release of more than 9,000 Cubans from the Guantanamo Naval Base put extreme pressure on IRP staff to find relocation and resettlement opportunities for those assigned to CWS. In addition, CWS resettled nearly 500 Haitians and continued its legal services program for Haitian asylum seekers in Florida and elsewhere. A new group that CWS worked hard to resettle were Bosnians requiring emergency medical attention.

******

The signing of a peace agreement in Dayton, Ohio, made it possible for CWS to begin moving from direct relief activities in the former Yugoslavia to making plans for reconstruction and development programs. Peter Mikuliak, a former CWS/CROP associate director in New Jersey with long experience in Eastern Europe and a member of the Orthodox Church in America, was assigned to work with local partners in Bosnia-Herzegovina on projects to help rebuild the economic life of communities. During 1995, through the CWS Europe Office, member communions, supplemented with CEFR public appeal funds, sent more than $416,000 in assistance to refugees and displaced persons in ten locations in Bosnia-Herzegovina. In addition, CWS responded with more than $1.75 million in emergency appeals for Armenia, Georgia, Russia, and Poland.

The "peace process" in the Middle East continued along an uncertain path during 1995. While there were positive signs, including the Palestinian elections and the redeployment of Israeli troops, bombing attacks and the resulting "security measures" caused much suffering. The events also frustrated those on both sides seeking a nonviolent resolution to a decades-old struggle. With help from Church World Service, its partner, the Middle East Council of Churches Department on Services to Palestinian Refugees (DSPR), worked in Gaza to provide vital emergency services of food and other needs to families facing poverty and hunger. At the same time, it attempted to maintain its ongoing programs of vocational training and basic health care. On the West Bank, mother-and-child health clinics of the DSPR became the primary medical resources of entire communities as restrictions on travel limited access to other facilities. Again, while having to provide emergency relief, the DSPR continued its work in development programs including land reclamation, housing rehabilitation, and education.

Both the CWS Latin America and Caribbean office and the Office on Development Policy were involved in the "Peace Process and Support for Indigenous Leaders in Guatemala." It has been estimated that in Guatemala, because of government repression, kidnappings, and assassinations, some 50,000 women have been widowed and 250,000 children left fatherless. In 1995, Church World Service—together with the World Council of Churches, the Latin American Council of Churches, and the Lutheran World Federation—held the Fourth Consultation on Peace between the government, the army, and the guerrillas in Guatemala. The Latin America and Caribbean office also played an important role in the physical and emotional recovery of indigenous women leaders who had been victims of oppression. Meanwhile, when CWS received word of death threats against colleagues in Guatemala, the ODP succeeded in persuading members of the U.S. Congress to send a letter to the President of Guatemala asking that he protect those threatened by violence. The resulting international attention worked to secure the safety of those CWS colleagues.

In Africa, Church World Service continued to bring hope to the people of Rwanda and to help churches with long-term development. After the Rwandan war and resulting genocide, more than 100,000 children were orphaned. To assist two of the most vulnerable groups in Rwanda, widows and orphans, CWS initiated its Family-to-Family Project. The primary goal of the project was to support widows who adopted orphans and to begin rebuilding a family structure in that country. In addition to the displaced persons in their own country, more than one quarter of a million Rwandan refugees remained in Tanzania, and three-quarters of a million were still in camps around Goma, Zaire. In 1995, CWS continued its work with the Christian Council of Tanzania, the Church of Christ in Zaire, and the United Nations High Commissioner for Refugees (UNHCR) in providing essential medical services for those refugees. Church World Service, meanwhile, was supporting the need for institutional stability and development in the Sudan Council of Churches and the Christian Council of Mozambique as they worked to serve the churches and people of their countries.

Following a tradition that goes back to the early days of CWS, theological students from many countries are still being brought to the United States to continue their studies. During 1995, four students from Indonesia, Kenya, and Germany were selected to study at the Episcopal Theological Seminary in Virginia. After completing their studies in theology and Christian education, they will return home to teach in their own churches and seminaries. At the same time, the China Program of the East Asia and Pacific Office made it possible for five pastors and theologians from the China Christian Council to study at various seminaries in the United States. During the past three years, CWS helped 120 students from twenty countries to do graduate study in the United States

In the mid-1990s, Church World Service continued its concern for the role of women as it had since its earlier "Consultation on Women and Development" held in India in the 1970s. Church World Service sponsored a delegation of seven women to the UN Fourth World Conference on Women, in Beijing, as well as sponsoring a women's gathering on the North American Free Trade

Agreement (NAFTA), in McAllen, Texas. Women of diverse backgrounds from the United States and Mexico met to focus on the impact of NAFTA on the lives of women in both countries.

******

In 1995, as they have for nearly a half-century, church members from many denominations, as well as the broader community, continued to support Church World Service through CROP Walks and other public appeals. More than 269,000 people took part in some 1,861 CROP Walks and eighty-five other interfaith, community events across the United States. Their combined efforts raised $13.9 million, 25 percent of which was shared with food banks, pantries, community gardens, and other local hunger-fighting agencies nationwide.

The Michigan CWS/CROP Region, where CROP Walks have been held every year for the past twenty-five years, became the first region to have an annual income of more than $2 million in 1995. David Bower, who served with CWS in Southern Asia before becoming a CWS/CROP regional director in 1970, has helped organize CROP events in cities and communities across the state for a quarter of a century.

Blankets continued to be in great demand. In 1995 more than 70,000 blankets were shipped internationally, with 47,500 of them going to Bosnia alone. In that same period, 196,440 health kits and 62,607 school kits were sent overseas; again the largest number went to war-torn former Yugoslavia. Also during that year, $2,681,987 in Blanket Program funds were sent to twenty-seven countries for the local purchase of blankets or material with which to make blankets or other bedding items. Whenever appropriate, CWS sends funds for the purchase of supplies to help the local economy and to provide employment, especially for women. It had also become the policy of CWS to use blanket funds not only for the purchase of blankets, but also to supply funds for temporary shelter needs such as plastic sheeting and tents.

During the 1980s and the early 1990s, domestic disasters and increasingly large numbers of homeless people in the United States made it necessary for CWS to make blankets and other supplies available to local churches and ecumenical agencies in larger amounts. Almost 25,000 wool and cotton blankets went to twenty-four states to be used by homeless people, refugees, and migrant workers. Other supplies sent to ecumenical agencies with large populations of refugees and migrants included health kits, food, baby blankets, school kits, and layettes. Special "cleanup" kits were sent to areas that had suffered a disaster, and included basic items to help the households recover from the devastation of a tornado, hurricane, or flood.

One example of how CWS blankets are bringing some comfort is seen in the joint program of CWS and "Midnight Run" of Dobbs Ferry, New York. Volunteers from local churches go into New York City three to four nights a week to distribute blankets and food. Last year, Midnight Run volunteers distributed 12,000 blankets, 8,000 from local churches, 4,000 from CWS. Another example is the New Jersey "Fellowship House" of the South Camden Christian Fellowship, which works with children from low-income families. Church World Service supplies woolen blankets to Fellowship House to help meet the needs of families living in poorly-maintained rental housing, often with little or no heat.

******

Church World Service saw no letup in new challenges in its Jubilee Year. Continued warfare, a poor harvest, and a bitter winter greeted the people of Chechnya in 1996. Church World Service provided $750,000, including more than $110,000 in Blanket Program funds, for the Action of Churches Together (ACT) a relief and rehabilitation program in Chechnya and surrounding republics. Flooding in the Republic of Korea (North Korea) caused $15 billion in damages. Hospitals, day-care centers, electric and communications facilities, bridges, and thousands of miles of roads were affected. Shortfalls in maize and rice production of almost two million tons were expected in 1996. Church World Service received licenses from the U.S. government to purchase and ship rice and medicines valued at $500,000 to North Korea; CWS also applied for an additional license to ship canned beef donated by the Church of the Brethren valued at $136,000. At the time of the floods in North Korea, CWS shipped antibiotics and rehydration tablets to assist in halting the spread of cholera. In February and March 1996, a second massive earthquake hit northwestern China, leaving hundreds of thousands homeless. Church World Service provided $178,000 to the Amity Foundation, CWS's partner in China, to help provide blankets, bedding, and temporary shelter for suffering earthquake survivors.

Africa was not spared. Fighting in and around Monrovia, Liberia, threatened a recurrence of the terrible humanitarian crisis of the early 1990s. Widespread food shortages already existed, and the international community, including the United States, was advising its citizens to evacuate the country in the face of the tragic situation there. Humanitarian-aid operations were virtually impossible, and CWS continued to monitor the situation through its partners in neighboring countries.

Real peace in the Middle East continued to prove elusive. The Israeli military campaign against Hezbollah guerrilla fighters continued, resulting in scores of deaths and injuries, and displacing some 400,000 people. Those remaining in southern Lebanon lived under the constant threat of shelling, and even those who sought safety in the UN-sponsored refugee camp were not spared when Israeli shells struck the camp and killed more than ninety Lebanese civilians.

In the United States, a devastating spring drought threatened up to 40 percent of the year's wheat harvest, while tornadoes and hurricanes in the southeast killed scores of people and destroyed the homes of thousands.

Ecumenical agencies continued to work with CWS/IRP to resettle newly-arrived refugees from many parts of the world.

Fifty years of help and hope . . . Facing challenges of a magnitude it is sometimes hard to imagine, Church World Service has made an immeasurable difference through the years. It was the faith and the determination of members of the U.S. churches who, in 1946, reached out to help the victims of the most destructive war the world has ever seen. Now, fifty years later, when millions are threatened by poverty and hunger, by oppressive governments and civil strife, by natural disasters that occur around the world, the sons and daughters and grandchildren of those who gave life to CWS initially are equally determined that in their own time they will show the love of God by responding to human need wherever it may be found.

CWS

Wheat from North Dakota Grain Growers Association sent through CWS, being distributed in Russia. 1992

UNHCR

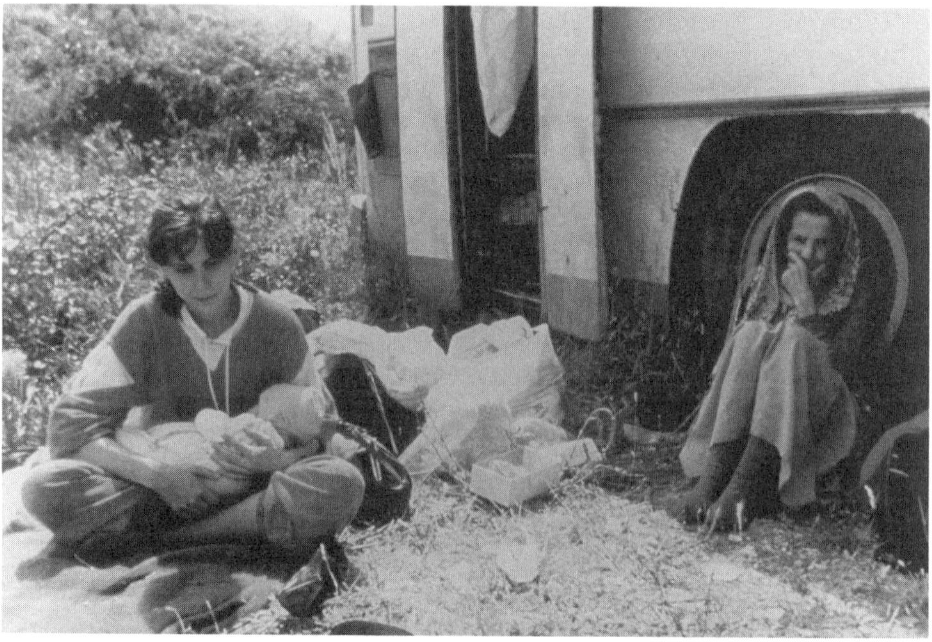

Refugee mother and child near city of Split, Croatia after fleeing fighting in Sarajevo, Bosnia-Herzegovina, in the former Yugoslavia. 1992

F. Daniel/CWS

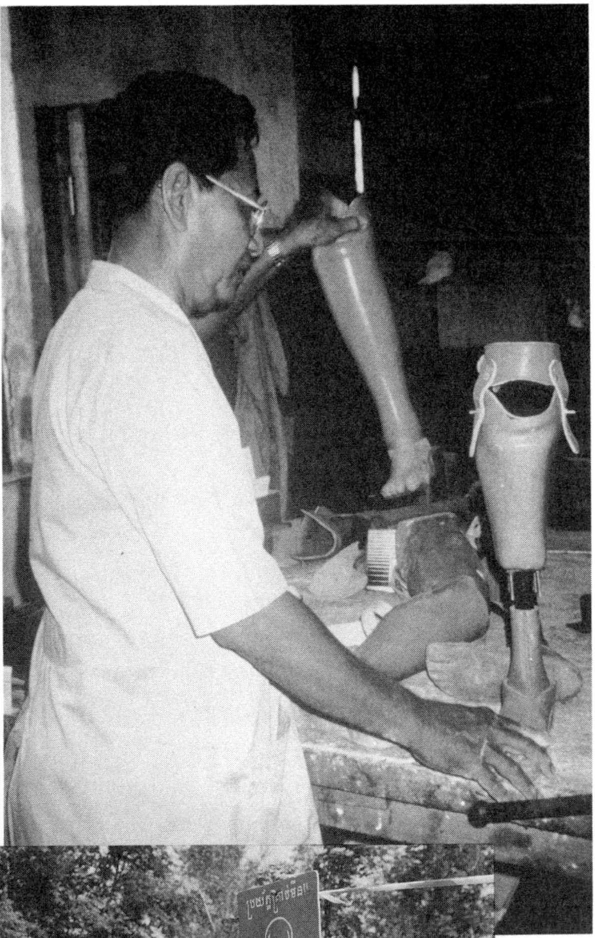

Making prostheses
for amputees
in Cambodia, in
a program supported
by CWS. 1994

CWS

Using a mine detector in an effort to find buried landmines
in Battambang, Cambodia. 1994

WCC

Young man in a Middle East Council of Churches center for vocational training in Gaza. 1990

CWS-CROP

Volunteers in a food pantry in northern New England, funded in part by 25 percent of the funds raised in a local CROP Walk and returned to the community to support local hunger programs. 1994

What does the Lord require of you but to do justice, and to love kindness, and to walk humbly with your God?

Micah 6:8 NRSV

Hope means more than just hanging on. It is the conscious decision to see the world in a different way than most others see it. To hope is to look . . . to a future not determined by the oppressive circumstances of the present.

Jim Wallis, Editor
Sojourners Magazine

Postscript

1996 and Beyond

As Church World Service moves toward the twenty-first century, ours is a very different world and a very different church from what existed when CWS was founded fifty years ago. It is a world of rapid social and political change, yet the urgency of responding to global human need is as real and as pressing as it was in 1946. Church World Service has new leadership both on staff and in its governing body. Lonnie Turnipseed has retired, and Rodney Page has become executive director. Belle Miller McMaster, of the Presbyterian Church (U.S.A.), has completed her term as chair of the Church World Service and Witness Committee, and Will L. Herzfeld, of the Evangelical Lutheran Church in America, has been elected to that position. They, along with staff and committees and thousands of volunteers, will lead Church World Service into the future.

No one can predict the future with certainty nor what that future will mean for Church World Service. Nevertheless, certain signs forecast the shape of the world in the early years of the twenty-first century.

Two reports released in May 1996, the fiftieth anniversary

month of Church World Service, suggested some issues the people of the world will face in the years immediately ahead. The Worldwatch Institute's report states that the world is becoming more crowded and food is scarcer. The world's grain harvest in 1995 was the smallest since 1988, and grain reserves were at an all-time low of just forty-eight days of consumption. The low grain reserve is made even more serious as the southwestern United States is experiencing a severe drought reminiscent of the Dust-Bowl days of the 1930s, a drought that will adversely affect the 1996 harvest.

Another concern reported by Worldwatch is an ever-increasing world population. The next decade will probably see close to an additional billion people in the developing world. Most of them will be born poor and grow to adulthood in poverty. The result may be increasing violence as ever more people compete for fewer and fewer resources. The availability of sophisticated weapons and the inability of political leaders to exercise effective control, may result in bloodbaths similar to those in Rwanda and Liberia. A glut of refugees fleeing the violence will put additional strain on the economies and social fabric of neighboring nations. During the Cold War, the superpowers maintained some level of order within their own spheres of influence. Yet with such control no longer effective, or even wanted, unrestrained violence has become endemic in many countries.

Another concern cited in a report by the World Health Organization (WHO) is that a combination of factors is producing a devastating spread of infectious diseases. Despite the good news that more children are immunized against measles and polio, 50,000 people die every day, seventeen million a year, from infectious diseases, and "there is no respite in sight," according to the WHO report. During the last twenty years, at least thirty new diseases have emerged to threaten the health of millions of people, and for many of them there is no treatment, cure, or vaccine, the report says.

Increasing poverty, overpopulation, ecological damage, and disintegration are all signs that the institutional and economic systems that have been in place for years are no longer working to the benefit of most of the world's people. The widening gap between the rich and the poor within and between nations has been well documented, not only in developing countries but also in the United States. Because of corporate downsizing, racism, and increasing homelessness, millions of people are shut out of the nation's economic system. Some members of Congress advocate public policies aimed at dismantling the safety-net for poor people, reducing funds for anti-poverty programs, making cuts in food stamps, and attacking programs of education and environmental protection. Internationally, cuts in funds for family planning, economic adjustment programs of the World Bank, and reductions in foreign aid are adversely affecting the world's poor people.

Present global realities will make the activities of an agency such as Church World Service increasingly important. That will be true not only in relation to its original threefold mandate (relief, development and refugees), but especially for its programs of global education and public policy advocacy. David Korten of the Institute for Development Research argues in his book, *The U.S. Voluntary Sector and Global Realities: Issues for the 1990s*, that in the years ahead, issues of international development will need to be cast in a fundamentally new light. "International development" he writes, "must be redefined to conform to the redefinition of the development task. It must become a two-way process in which information, not money is the primary medium of exchange." He goes on to say that voluntary organizations have a particular role to play in global education and in performing advocacy functions with governments and international bodies. Korten believes that international agencies will be needed to provide humanitarian assistance that helps the victims of human disasters often caused by the failure of global economic systems. However, greater emphasis needs to be placed on helping people in developed countries understand the reasons for that failure. Such an approach clearly calls for a continuation of CWS's programs of relief, development, and refugee assistance, but also for an increased emphasis on global education and public policy advocacy—actions called for by the participants in the Fortieth Anniversary Symposium a decade ago.

Korten makes another point that is crucial to the future of CWS. Private Voluntary Organizations (PVOs) need to build partnerships with indigenous nongovernmental agencies (NGOs). The CWS Latin America and Caribbean Office, through the São Paulo Process, has already moved in that direction. By doing that, it has shown a concern for mutual sharing with indigenous groups and has based its development strategies on an understanding of local conditions. In contrast to fifty years ago, when taking the lead in establishing overseas operations and programs was necessary for CWS, many parts of Latin America, Asia, and Africa have well-established NGOs. As it moves into the future, a pattern similar to the São Paulo Process will become, hopefully, the model followed increasingly by CWS.

However, it is not only the world, and the ways an agency responds to human need in the world, that has changed in the past fifty years. The churches and the PVO community have changed as well. The U.S. religious consensus of the past—of Protestants, Catholics, and Jews—clearly no longer exists. Immigration, intermarriages, and conversions have brought a new diversity onto the stage. Hindus, Moslems, and Buddhists have contributed to the religious fabric of the United States in increasing numbers, with some evidence suggesting that by the next generation Islam may be the second largest religion in the United States. There are new players on both the domestic and international scene, and the NCCC/CWS must recognize that interreligious understanding and constructive cooperation between denominations, agencies, and various religious groups in the United States and in other countries is more important than ever before. Institutional ecumenism is less important to some denominations than it was in the past, yet local grassroots ecumenism, as demonstrated in CROP Walks and similar events, is healthy and flourishing.

The PVO community has also changed dramatically. Only a few years ago, the few members of the American Council of Voluntary Agencies in Foreign Service (now called InterAction) represented most of the work being done by PVOs. Today there are more than one hundred agency members of InterAction involved in programs of relief, development, refugee resettlement, education, and advocacy in one way or another.

Competition for public funds is becoming much more intense. Many newer organizations are using activities pioneered by CROP, such as walks and other sponsored events, to raise funds. As CWS becomes increasingly dependent on its Community Education and Fund-Raising program (CEFR) for financial support, it will be important for denominational leaders and local clergy to inform their members that Church World Service is *their* agency, and that by participating in CROP Walks and other events, they are supporting programs and activities that benefit their denominational programs.

Church life in the United States is significantly different today than it was fifty years ago because of the commitment of those who helped establish Church World Service. Their decision to respond to God's call to work together and to take seriously the call to respond to human need has enabled CWS to stand with and support partners around the world. In many ways, the future of Church World Service will depend on renewing the ecumenical commitment of its member churches to continue to work together as partners, rather than developing their own bilateral programs as some larger denominations have begun to do.

Church World Service has committed itself to a ministry of service and of bringing help and hope into the lives of millions. It has exercised a ministry of healing and reconciliation, serving people in need throughout the world. As it moves ahead into more complex times, with ever increasing situations of human need, it will be called upon to stand in solidarity with those who seek justice. It will face difficult and often imperfect choices as it has often in the past. Predicting the future with any certainty is always an impossible task, but if the past is any guide, those difficult and often imperfect choices will be made.

An audiovisual presentation was produced by Linda Robbins at the time of the fortieth anniversary of CWS. On the final slide of that presentation were the words:

"To Be Continued"

As Church World Service and its member denominations look toward the future there can be no better nor more important charge than that.

END NOTES

PART ONE 1946–1956

1. Original denominations of Church World Service: Christian Churches (Disciples of Christ), Church of the Brethren, Congregational Christian Churches, Evangelical and Reformed, Evangelical Congregational, Evangelical United Brethren, Friends Five Year Meeting, National Lutheran Council, Northern Baptist Convention, Presbyterian in the U.S.A., Seventh Day Baptist, Southern Baptist Convention, The Methodist Church, The Reformed Church of America, The Episcopal Church, United Presbyterian.
2. Phillips, Cabell, *Decade of Triumph and Trouble* (New York: MacMillan Publishing Co., Inc., 1975).
3. *The Christian Century,* April 1948.
4. *The Christian Century,* September 1957.
5. Ekin, Larry, *Enduring Witness: The Churches and the Palestinians* (Geneva: World Council of Churches, 1985).
6. Fey, Harold E., *Cooperation in Compassion* (New York: Friendship Press, 1966).
7. Ibid., 37.
8. Letters from early volunteers.
9. Fey, 64.
10. Ibid., 72.
11. Ibid., 70.
12. *The Christian Century,* May, 1950.

PART TWO 1957–1966

1. New York University Conference on Immigration, June, 1953.
2. *The Christian Century,* 1957.
3. *The Christian Century,* 1955.
4. Letter from John Backer.
5. Fey, 99.
6. Ekin, 17.
7. Fey, 109.
8. Ibid., 113.
9. Letter from James MacCracken.
10. Knight, Doris, *Church World Service: The Power of the Humanitarian Ideal* (Omaha: Creighton University, 1984), 65.
11. Letter from James MacCracken.
12. Ekin, 27.
13. Fey, 131.
14. Church World Service, *Witness in Anguish: Vietnam Christian Service* (New York: Church World Service, 1976), 30.
15. Ibid., Boyd Lowry, Preface.
16. Fey, 156.
17. "Community Compassion," CROP Information Services, 1967.

PART THREE 1967–1976

1. *The Christian Century,* March 1965.
2. Chad, Mali, Mauritania, Niger, Senegal, Upper Volta.
3. James MacCracken, Annual Report, Division of Overseas Ministries, 1969.
4. Letter from Gary Ambrose.
5. *Witness in Anguish,* 49.
6. Letter from John Metzler, Jr.
7. Burtner, Roger, "Pages From a Pilgrim's Journey, Report on Volunteers in Mission," CWS African Travel Seminar, 1973, 9.
8. Aaker, Jerry, *Partners With the Poor* (New York: Friendship Press, 1993), 26.
9. Ibid., 34.
10. Haines, J. Harry, *World Without Hunger* (New York: Church World Service, 1976), 16.
11. CWS Consultation, Stony Point, New York (June 20–21, 1973).
12. "Worldview,"quoted in *The Christian Century,* 1975.
13. Haines, 53.
14. Ohio, Michigan, Western Pennsylvania, Indiana.
15. Stenning, Ronald E., "The Fourth Decade," written for the National CROP Committee, 1976.

PART FOUR 1977–1986

1. Haines, 57.
2. Dickinson, Richard D. N., *Poor Yet Making Many Rich* (Geneva: World Council of Churches, 1983), 93.
3. *American Wheat, Destination Vietnam,* 16mm film, produced by Church World Service, 1979.
4. CWS Annual Report, 1980.
5. CWS World Hunger Fact Sheet, Number 15, 1980.
6. Letter from Larry Hollon.
7. Kimball, Charles, *Striving Together: A Way Forward in Christian-Muslim Relations* (Maryknoll, NY: Orbis, 1991).
8. Knight, 117.

PART FIVE 1987–1996

1. OGE Reprint Series.
2. 40th Anniversary Report, 2nd Cut; Hugh Wire.
3. CWS Annual Report, 1988.
4. *For the Healing of the Nations—Thirty Daily Devotions,* CWS Office on Global Education, 1996, Day 2.
5. Ibid., Day 20.
6. CWS Annual Report, 1988.
7. CWS Annual Report, 1989.
8. CWS Annual Report, 1990.
9. Beardslee, Ann, Report to the Unit Committee, February 1990.
10. Letter from Dale Bishop.
11. Ibid.
12. CWSW Annual Report, 1992.
13. CWSW Annual Report, 1993.
14. Hollon, Larry, "Storyline" a publication of Larry Hollon Communications Group, Stroud, OK, Vol.1, No.3, 1995.
15. *For the Healing of the Nations,* Day 21.

APPENDIXES

APPENDIX A

Church World Service Constituent Communions

African Methodist Episcopal Church

African Methodist Episcopal Zion Church

American Baptist Churches USA

The Antiochian Orthodox Christian Archdiocese of North America

Armenian Church of America (including Diocese of California)

Christian Church (Disciples of Christ)

Christian Methodist Episcopal Church

Church of the Brethren

The Coptic Orthodox Church in North America

The Episcopal Church

Evangelical Lutheran Church in America

Friends United Meeting

Greek Orthodox Archdiocese of North and South America

Hungarian Reformed Church in America

International Council of Community Churches

Korean Presbyterian Church in America

Moravian Church in America

National Baptist Convention of America

National Baptist Convention, U.S.A., Inc.

National Missionary Baptist Convention of America

Orthodox Church in America

Patriarchal Parishes of the Russian Orthodox Church in the U.S.A.

Philadelphia Yearly Meeting of the Religious Society of Friends

Polish National Catholic Church of America

Presbyterian Church (U.S.A.)

Progressive National Baptist Convention, Inc.

Reformed Church in America

Serbian Eastern Orthodox Church in the U.S.A. and Canada

The Swedenborgian Church

Syrian Orthodox Church of Antioch

Ukrainian Orthodox Church in America

United Church of Christ

The United Methodist Church

APPENDIX B

Church World Service
Key Addresses and Contact Numbers

Church World Service
Church World Service and Witness
475 Riverside Dr., Rm. 678
New York, NY 10115-0050
(212) 870-2257; (212) 870-2055 (fax)

For most inquiries and for the CWS Film & Video Library:
Church World Service
Community Education and Fund Raising Program
28606 Phillips St.
P.O. Box 968
Elkhart, IN 46515
(219) 264-3102; (219) 262-0966 (fax)

Church World Service
Immigration and Refugee Program
475 Riverside Dr., Rm. 652
New York, NY 10115-0050
(212) 870-3300; (212) 870-2132 (fax)

Church World Service
Office on Global Education
2115 N. Charles St.
Baltimore, MD 21218-5755
(410) 727-6106; (210) 727-6108 (fax)

CWS/LWR
Office on Development Policy
Building Box 45
110 Maryland Ave., NE, Ste. 108
Washington, DC 20002
(202) 543-6336; (202) 546-6232 (fax)

Church World Service HOTLINE
(800) 465-1310—for a recorded message about
CWS emergency response and programs

Church World Service PLEDGE LINE
(800) 762-0968

APPENDIX C

Church World Service/CROP U.S. Regional Offices

CHURCH WORLD SERVICE COMMUNITY EDUCATION AND FUND RAISING PROGRAM
28606 Phillips St.
P.O. Box 968
Elkhart, IN 46515
(219) 264-3102
(219) 262-0966 (fax)

CAROLINAS
1006 Lamond Ave.
Durham, NC 27701
(919) 688–3843

CHICAGO/NORTHERN ILLINOIS
900 Jorie Blvd., Ste. 32
Oak Brook, IL 60521
(630) 990–7441

PENNSYLVANIA
3913 Market St.
Camp Hill, PA 17011
(717) 761–8180

FLORIDA
934 N. Magnolia, Ste. 110
Orlando, FL 32803
(407) 426–7123

GREAT PLAINS
2905 1/2 S. W. 29th St.
Topeka, KS 66614
(913) 272–8322

ILLINOIS
503 E. St. Joseph St.
Springfield, IL 62703
(217) 529–5144

INDIANA (KENTUCKY)
1100 W. 42nd St.
Indianapolis, IN 46208
(317) 923–2938

IOWA
3816 36th St., Ste. 203
Des Moines, IA 50310
(515) 274–2224

MICHIGAN
Oakland Center, Ste. 7A
809 Center St.
P.O. Box 10206
Lansing, MI 48901
(517) 484–7144

MID-ATLANTIC
Ste. 112
4920 Niagara Rd.
College Park, MD 20740
(301) 441–1676

MINN-KOTA
122 W. Franklin, Rm. 4
Minneapolis, MN 55404
(612) 872–7332

MISSOURI
1803 Sun Valley Dr., Ste. B
P.O. Box 1073
Jefferson City, MO 65102
(573) 635–1012

NEW JERSEY
125 Washington St.
P.O. Box 214
Rocky Hill, NJ 08553
(609) 924–6466

NEW YORK (UPSTATE)
Church Center
3049 E. Genesee St.
Syracuse, NY 13224
(315) 445–9055

NORTHERN CALIFORNIA
1401 21st St., Ste. 320
Sacramento, CA 95814
(916) 448–5917

NORTHERN NEW ENGLAND
733 Chapin St., Ste. 102
P.O. Box 381
Ludlow, MA 01056
(413) 583–8355

OHIO
3963 Cleveland Ave.
Columbus, OH 43224
(614) 471–1188

PACIFIC NORTHWEST
Garden Court Bldg.
Ste. 224
West 222 Mission Ave.
Spokane, WA 99201
(509) 328–8720

PACIFIC SOUTHWEST
1507 Garfield Ave.
South Pasadena, CA 91030
(818) 441–2827

ROCKY MOUNTAIN
Ste. 102
13741 E. Mississippi
Aurora, CO 80012
(303) 367–4980

TEXAS
Ste. 200
6633 Highway 290, E.
Austin, TX 78723
(512) 451–2062

TRI-STATE
7 Park Ave., Ste. 6
P.O. Box 177
Colchester, CT 06415
(860) 537–0679

VIRGINIA/WEST VIRGINIA
1627 Monument Ave.
3rd Fl.
Richmond, VA 23220
(804) 355–4642

WISCONSIN
1955 W. Broadway, Ste. 102
Madison, WI 53713
(608) 222–7008

APPENDIX D

Church World Service Immigration and Refugee Program Contact List

CHURCH WORLD SERVICE
IMMIGRATION AND REFUGEE PROGRAM
475 Riverside Dr., Rm. 652
New York, NY 10115–0050
(212) 870–3300
(212) 870–2132 (fax)

Ecumenical Refugee Resttlement and Sponsorship Services (ERRS) Affliate Offices of CWS/IRP

ARIZONA

Central Arizona Refugee Ecumenical Service (CARES)
4423 N. 24th St., Rm. 510
Phoenix, AZ 85016
(602) 956–7556

CALIFORNIA

Refugee Assistance Program
3295 Meade Ave.
San Diego, CA 92116
(619) 284–1184

St. Anselm's Cross Cultural Community Center Refugee Program
13091 Galway St.
Garden Grove, CA 92844
(714) 537–0608

St. Anselm's Cross Cultural Community Center Refugee Program sub–office
5250 Santa Monica Blvd., Rm. 305
Los Angeles, CA 90029
(213) 667–0489

Sacramento Refugee Ministry
2117 Cottage Way
Sacramento, CA 95825–1064
(916) 568–5020

COLORADO

Ecumenical Refugee Services, Inc.
190 East 9th Ave., Ste. 420
Denver, CO 80203
(303) 860–0666

CONNECTICUT

Episcopal Social Services, Inc. Interfaith Refugee Ministry
P.O. Box 8477
New Haven, CT 06530
(203) 562–2095

FLORIDA

Church World Service Miami Office
701 S.W. 27th Ave., Rm. 707
Miami, FL 33135
(305) 541–8040/41

Florida Council of Churches Refugee Program
924 N. Magnolia Ave.
Ste. 236, Orlando, FL 32803
(407) 839–3454

GEORGIA

Christian Council of Metropolitan Atlanta Refugee & Immigrant Resettlement Services
4173 Chapel Valley Dr.
Douglasville, GA 30135
(404) 622–2235

ILLINOIS

Interchurch Refugee & Immigration Ministries (IRIM)
4753 N. Broadway, Ste. 401
Chicago, IL 60640
(312) 989–5647

INDIANA

Exodus Refugee & Immigration Program, Inc.
701 N. Delaware St.
Indianapolis, IN 46204
(317) 238–0836

KENTUCKY

Kentucky Refugee Ministries, Inc.
1011 Cherokee Rd.
Louisville, KY 40204
(502) 452–9055

MARYLAND

World Ministries Commission of the Church of the Brethren

P.O. Box 188
500 Main St.
New Windsor, MD 21776–0188
(410) 635–8731/30

MICHIGAN

Freedom Flight Task Force

734 Alger, SE
Grand Rapids, MI 49507
(616) 241–5988

MINNESOTA

Minnesota Council of Churches (MCC) Refugee Services

122 W. Franklin, Rm. 7
Minneapolis, MN 55404
(612) 874–8605

NEBRASKA

Interchurch Ministries of Nebraska Nebraska Ecumenical Refugee & Sponsorship Program

215 Centennial Mall South, Ste. 411
Lincoln, NE 68508–1888
(402) 476–3391/3576

NEW YORK

Interfaith Community Services New York/New Jersey ERRSS

308 W. 46 Street, 3rd Fl.
New York, NY 10036
(212) 265–1826

Greater Rochester Community Churches Refugee Resettlement & Services Project

350 Chili Ave.
Rochester, NY 14611
(716) 528–2030

Interreligious Council of Central New York Refugee Resettlement Program

3049 East Genesee St.
Syracuse, NY 13224
(315) 474–1261/1262

Interreligious Council of Central New York Capital District Office

c/o Emmanuel Baptist Church
218 Nott Terrace
Schenectady, NY 12307
(518) 370–2995

Refugee Resettlement Office Binghamton Sub–Office

30 Main St.
Binghamton, NY 13905
(607) 773–0622

Ithaca Refugee Office Syracuse sub–office First Baptist Church De Witt Park

Box 254
Ithaca, NY 14850
(607) 277–8648

NORTH CAROLINA

Lutheran Family Services in the Carolinas, Inc.

415 N. Edgeworth St., Ste. 200
Greensboro, NC 27407
(910) 738–7881

Lutheran Family Services in the Carolinas, Inc., sub–office

505 Oberlin Road, Ste. 230
Raleigh, NC 27605
(919) 832–2620

SOUTH CAROLINA

Lutheran Family Services in the Carolinas, Inc., sub–office

P.O. Box 21728
1329 Atlantic Dr.
Columbia, SC 29221
(803) 731–9620

OHIO

Interfaith Refugee Services of Ohio (IRSO)

5303 N. High Street, Ste. D
Columbus, OH 43214
(614) 841–4975

OREGON

Ecumenical Ministries of Oregon
Sponsors Organized to Assist Refugees (SOAR)
5404 NE Alameda Dr.
Portland, OR 97213
(503) 284–3002

Idaho Office: SOAR
950 W. State St.
Boise, ID 83702
(208) 343–6633

PENNSYLVANIA PRIME

Ecumenical Commitment to Refugees
360 N. Oak Ave.
Clifton Heights, PA 19018
(610) 259–4500

PRIME sub–office
701 N. Lime St.
Lancaster, PA 17602
(717) 396–9300

TENNESSEE

Bridge Refugee and Sponsorship Services, Inc.
200 Lockett Rd.
Knoxville, TN 37919
(423) 588–2754

Bridge Refugee and Sponsorship Services, Inc.
sub–office
701 Florida Ave.
Bristol, TN 37620
(423) 652–1588

Bridge Refugee and Sponsorship Services, Inc.
sub–office
3113 Rose Terrace
Chattanooga, TN 37404
(423) 785–8208

Mid–Cumberland Refugee Assistance Ministry
3900 West End Ave.
Nashville, TN 37205
(615) 383–3772

TEXAS

Refugee Services of North Texas
4113 Junius
Dallas, TX 75246
(214) 821–4883

Interfaith Ministries for Greater Houston
IM Refugee Services
3217 Montrose Blvd.
Houston, TX 77006–3980
(713) 520–4637

Austin–Travis County Refugee Services
5555 N. Lamar, K–100
Austin, TX 78751
(512) 467–9816

VIRGINIA

Community Refugee Ecumenical Outreach (CREO)
2315 S. Grant St.
Arlington, VA 22202
(703) 979–5180

Virginia Council of Churches
Refugee Resettlement Program,
1214 W. Graham Rd., Ste. 3
Richmond, VA 23220
(804) 321–3305

Harrisonburg Refugee Resettlement Program
Richmond sub–office
731C E. Market St.
Harrisonburg, VA 22801
(703) 433–7942

Manassas Office
Manassas Baptist Church
8800 Sudley Rd.
Manassas, VA 22110
(703) 369–6101

WASHINGTON

Washington Refugee Resettlement
464 12th Ave., Ste. 220
Seattle, WA 98122
(206) 322–0409

INDEX